Etty Hillesum was born in 1914 into a family of privileged Dutch Jews. She was twenty-nine years old when she died.

ETTY: A DIARY 1941–43

'This is an ennobling and uplifting book, illuminated by self-tormenting yet touchingly beautiful prayers. . . Etty's Diary could become . . . one of the most important documents of our time.'
Stephen Corin, *Daily Telegraph*

'Another forceful indictment of ruthless Nazi terror . . . Her writing is infused with a remarkable faith and confidence in God and humanity.'
Brian Martin, *New Statesman*

'It is an extraordinary human document, so extraordinary in fact that I had to pause every now and again to ask if it could be authentic. By the end I felt it didn't matter for if this is a work of fiction it is a work of such imagination and power as to have the validity of fact . . . I have been torn by conflicting emotions in reading this book, but finally put it down with a feeling of awe. Like Job, *Etty* revives one's faith in man, though it diminishes one's faith in God.'
Chaim Bermant, *Times Literary Supplement*

D0779806

By the same author

Etty: A Diary 1941–43

ETTY HILLESUM

Letters from Westerbork

Introduction and notes by Jan G. Gaarlandt

Translation by Arnold J. Pomerans

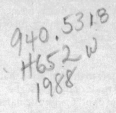

GRAFTON BOOKS

A Division of the Collins Publishing Group

LONDON GLASGOW
TORONTO SYDNEY AUCKLAND

Grafton Books
A Division of the Collins Publishing Group
8 Grafton Street, London W1X 3LA

Published by Grafton Books 1988

First published in Great Britain by
Jonathan Cape Ltd 1987

Originally published in the Netherlands as *Het denkende
hart van de barak* by De Haan/Unieboeck b.v., Bussum

English translation copyright © Random House Inc 1986
Copyright © De Haan/Unieboeck b.v., Bussum 1982

ISBN 0-586-07244-6

Printed and bound in Great Britain by
Collins, Glasgow

Set in Times

*Thanks to Leigh Hafrey for translating the
Rilke passage on pages 11–12.
Special thanks to Dr. Gerd Korman for the
photograph of his father, Osias Kormann.*

t

At night the barracks sometimes lay in the moonlight, made out of silver and eternity: like a plaything that had slipped from God's preoccupied hand.

Etty's diary, 23 September 1942

CONTENTS

INTRODUCTION

"... *And the endless trek through the barracks and the mud began all over again.*"

As Etty Hillesum wrote in one of her many letters to friends during 1942 and 1943, mud and misery were the essence of Westerbork concentration camp. Also sickness, overcrowding, a whole world of noise and fear crammed into a patch of heath half a kilometer square.

Westerbork, a transit camp near Assen in the northeastern Netherlands, was "the last stop before Auschwitz" for more than one hundred thousand Dutch Jews. There Etty Hillesum spent the last months of her life, continuing to keep her diary, to write her letters, and, with great devotion, to nurse the sick in the hospital barracks. And it was in this hell that she wrote again and again, "Despite everything, life is full of beauty and meaning"—a characteristic affirmation that will be recognized immediately by readers of Etty's diaries.

Born on 15 January 1914, Etty Hillesum was twenty-seven years old when she began her diary in March 1941. At her desk in a small room overlooking Museum Square in Amsterdam, she produced one of the most remarkable texts of our time—a testimony of faith and love written in the darkest hours of modern history. Despite the growing horror of the German occupation and the persecution of the Jews, she tried, together with her friends and her lover Julius Spier, to build a defense against the forces bent on their destruction.

In 1942, the Germans launched their first major round-ups of the Jews, required them to wear the yellow star, and, after moving all the Jews they could find to Amsterdam, declared the provinces "*judenrein.*" The ultimate German objective, to transfer all Dutch Jews as smoothly as possible to extermination camps in Poland, depended on the cooperation of a specially created Jewish Council. The Germans set up similar councils, administered by leaders of the Jewish community, throughout occupied Europe. Their real purpose was to lull the fears of the panic-stricken Jews; their declared purpose was to decide who was fit to be sent away for "labor service" and who was indispensable at home.

A discussion of the role of the Jewish Council in the Netherlands falls outside the scope of this introduction, nor is this the place to pass judgment on it. What is relevant is that in July 1942, Etty was given a post in one of the many sections of the Jewish Council. The job exempted her from internment at Westerbork. Nonetheless, a few weeks later, she volunteered to go there as a "social worker." She arrived just as the remorseless rhythm of deportations to Auschwitz was beginning. Every Monday a train pulled into the camp; every Tuesday the long line of freight cars pulled out again, packed with more than a thousand men, women, boys, girls, infants, and the dying. From 15 July 1942 until 3 September 1944, week in, week out, the trains left, ninety-three in all.

The Jews in Amsterdam, who had been crowded into a ghetto during the previous months, were now sent to Westerbork. Some reported voluntarily; the rest were picked up in the streets or dragged out of their houses. From other prison and labor camps, too—for instance, the notorious camp in Vught and the ones in Amersfoort, Ommen, and Ellecom—Jews were packed off to Westerbork.

The exceptions were a small number of "cultural Jews"—intellectuals, artists, even bankers—who, at the intercession of a few high Dutch officials, could be assigned to a castle in the small town of Barneveld. Mischa, Etty's brother, a brilliant pianist, was eligible for Barneveld, but he refused to go without his parents. (Later all the Jews in this refuge were sent to Theresienstadt via Westerbork, and most survived.)

Westerbork was built at the end of 1939 by the Dutch government to house some fifteen hundred German Jews who had fled to the Netherlands before the war. Etty arrived in Westerbork just as the human landslide began, when room suddenly had to be found on the small site for thirty or forty thousand people. The aim of each one of these people, clutching the "stamps" the Jewish Council had issued to them, was to remain in Westerbork as long as possible. The stamps entitled them to stay a little longer in the camp—a week, two weeks, occasionally a few months. But in the long run, all stampholders disappeared—including the Jewish Council, most of whose members were deported in June 1943.

Westerbork had its own hierarchy, its own camp leaders, guards, medical staff, cultural officers, and so on—first under Dutch supervision, and then under German control. Among the inmates, the German-speaking Jews who had been in the camp for some years enjoyed the greatest influence.

One of these was Osias Kormann, who became Etty's close friend. It was to him that she wrote a number of letters in German from Amsterdam, where, after five weeks in Westerbork, and a short stay with her parents at Deventer, she had returned on 5 September. As a member of the Jewish Council, she held a travel permit that allowed her to return to Amsterdam occasionally in order to collect medical supplies and bring news to the families of people in the camp.

Etty stayed in Amsterdam for almost three months. Most of the time she spent in bed, ill, suffering, and even homesick for Westerbork. She returned to the camp on 20 November 1942, but two weeks later went back to Amsterdam and was admitted to the Netherlands Israelite Hospital to be treated for gallstones. Finally, early in June 1943, she left Amsterdam for Westerbork again, this time not to return. Her lover, the psychochirologist Julius Spier, had died; and she took her last leave of her close friends. It was to them that most of her letters from Westerbork were addressed, and readers of Etty's diary will know them: Han Wegerif ("Father Han"), the man in whose house she had been living and with whom she had had an intimate relationship, his son Hans, the housekeeper Käthe, and Maria Tuinzing, a nurse with whom Etty had grown particularly close the year before.

Then there were Tide (Henny Tideman), Klaas Smelik, his daughter Jopie (Johanna Smelik), Milli Ortmann, and finally Christine van Nooten from Deventer, a colleague of Etty's father, Louis Hillesum, who had been headmaster of Deventer Gymnasium. It was above all Milli Ortmann and Christine van Nooten who, through the Red Cross, kept sending food parcels to the Hillesums in Westerbork.

Whether Etty writes from Amsterdam or from the camp barracks, Westerbork is the all-embracing subject of this book. As she put it in one of the last entries in her diary, she wanted to be the "thinking heart of the barracks." And she was. She fired the imagination of many camp inmates; survivors still speak of her "shining personality." Wherever she was, she attracted a community of human fellowship. So it is not surprising that her letters reveal the growth of a whole new circle of close Westerbork friends: Osias Kormann, Werner Sterzenbach, Hedwig and Jupp Mahler, Jopie Vleeschhouwer, whom she called her "comrade-in-arms," Philip Mechanicus, author of *In Depôt*, a diary that became famous after the war, and, of course, Werner and Liesl Levie, old friends from Amsterdam. In time, they were joined by Etty's parents and her brother Mischa. Etty's other brother, Jaap, was allowed to remain in Amsterdam for a while because he was a doctor.

It was in this circle that Etty Hillesum displayed her courage and humanity. In Westerbork her soul found its deepest expression: she placed herself unreservedly at the service of her people. She spurned all attempts by her Amsterdam friends to take her to a safe address (on one occasion, by force) during the time she was still permitted to travel; she rejected all offers to help her escape from the camp when, after June 1943, she was no longer allowed to leave it. She was determined to share the fate of her fellow Jews, without bravado but also without despair. "Poland" to her was synonymous with destruction; she did not delude herself on that score. She knew that she would not survive, although she tried to calm her friends by predicting her return. How death would come to her she did not know. No one in Westerbork had heard about the gas chambers, but many knew intuitively that their fate was sealed.

On 7 September 1943, following a sudden order putting

Mischa, Etty, and her parents on the next transport to Poland, Etty stepped onto the platform beside the waiting train. Jopie Vleeschhouwer described her departure in a letter to the friends in Amsterdam: "Talking gaily, smiling, a kind word for everyone she met on the way, full of sparkling humor, perhaps just a touch of sadness, but every inch the Etty you all know so well. . . . I saw Mother, Father H., and Mischa board car No. 1. Etty finished up in No. 12, having first stopped to look for a friend in car No. 14, who was pulled out again at the last minute. Then a shrill whistle and the 1,000 'transport cases' were moving out. Another flourish from Mischa, who waved through a crack in No. 1, a cheerful ''Bye' from Etty in No. 12, and they were gone."

The journey was to last three days. Before they finally left the Netherlands, Etty threw a postcard addressed to Christine van Nooten out of the train: "We left the camp singing." They reached Auschwitz on 10 September 1943. That very day, her father and mother were gassed.

On 30 November 1943, the Red Cross reported the death of Etty Hillesum. Her brother Mischa died on 31 March 1944. Jaap was finally sent to Westerbork at the beginning of 1944. He, too, did not survive the war.

Etty Hillesum's letters came into my possession in 1980, when Dr. K. A. D. Smelik handed them to me together with the notebooks containing Etty's diaries. He had been authorized to do so by his father, Klaas Smelik, and his half-sister, Johanna Smelik. The Smelik family had acquired the papers in 1946 from Maria Tuinzing. Most of the letters, which had circulated among Etty's friends during the war, had eventually ended up in Maria's hands. Two long letters from the camp—those of December 1942 and 24 August 1943—had been clandestinely published at the end of 1943 in book form by the Dutch resistance.

For years after the war, the Smelik family tried to find a publisher for the diaries, but in vain. Finally in 1981 I was privileged to publish them. Now, owing to worldwide interest (the diaries have been translated into English, French, German, Italian, Spanish, Swedish, Norwegian, Danish, Finnish, Portuguese, Hebrew, and Japanese), research into Etty's life has expanded. As a result, a number of new letters have come to light. The most important group was handed to me by Professor Gerd Korman, a historian at Cornell University. Korman had learned about Etty's diaries and remembered some letters left by his late father, Osias Kormann. I am particularly indebted to Gerd Korman for giving permission to publish the letters Etty wrote to his father. (Korman's account of the friendship between his father and Etty will be found in note 3, at the end of this book.) Then, shortly before the English edition of the letters went to press, five more letters were discovered in the estate of Mrs. Grete Wendelsgelst. They had been written by Etty to Grete's sister, Milli Ortmann. I am grateful for the opportunity to include these letters in the present collection. I also received another ten letters and postcards for publication from Mrs. J. C. J. C. van Nooten, to whom I am also greatly indebted. It is certainly possible that still more letters will come to light; during the last months of her life Etty probably wrote over a hundred. But there will be no more diaries; Etty took her last notebook with her on the train to Auschwitz.

In conclusion, I would draw the reader's attention to the work of the Etty Hillesum Foundation in Amsterdam, under whose auspices her collected writings will be published toward the end of 1986. It is in part thanks to this foundation that I have been able to present the English edition of Etty's letters in as authoritative a form as possible. No changes have been made in the style or contents of the letters; only the punctuation and the spelling have been slightly modified. Nor has anything been omitted. Where amplification has seemed essential, it has been placed in brackets. This has applied particularly to the names of the recipients, and the dates of the letters.

Jan G. Gaarlandt
Haarlem, March 1986

LETTERS FROM WESTERBORK

Wednesday, 2:00 p.m.[1]

My heart failed a few times again today, but each time it came back to life. I say my good-byes from minute to minute, shaking myself free of all outer things. I cut through the ropes that still hold me bound, I load up with everything I need to set out on my journey. I am sitting now by a quiet canal, my legs dangling over the stone wall, and I wonder whether one day my heart will be so weary and worn that it will no longer fly where it wants, free as a bird.

AMSTERDAM

6 Gabriel Metsustraat,[2] Amsterdam, 14 August 1942

My good and dear friend Kormann,[3]

A little greeting from this big city. As I walk through the far too many streets here, Westerbork is always with me. It is strange that in such a short time a person can come to feel so much at one with a place and its inhabitants. I will be glad to get back there, even though I find it hard to leave those who are close to me here. But I feel somehow impelled to return to that spot in the middle of the heath where so many human destinies have been thrown together. I cannot explain to myself why this should be. Perhaps it will become clear to me later, but anyway, I shall be coming back. The man who is closest to me needs to recover slowly and patiently.[4] There is something wrong with his lungs and it will be a long and weary business. He is being lovingly cared for here; I can do nothing more for him, so I can go away for another few weeks with an easy conscience. Tomorrow I shall try to get a travel permit to visit my parents in Deventer; they miss me very much. If I succeed, I shall not be able to get to Westerbork before Thursday. Please don't think me faithless. And please make me another pudding when I do come. This time I shall make sure my stomach is up to it.

It is now eight o'clock and I am sitting at my desk, where I hope to spend a long and peaceful evening seeing to all sorts of things. Please remember me to your nice roommate, Herr Haussmann, and to other friends, and very best wishes to you yourself, from

Etty Hillesum

Kormann, my good friend,

You know, everything is so mysterious and strange, and so full of meaning, too.

My friend has died; I heard the news a few hours ago. Ever since I saw him last week, I have prayed that he might be released from his suffering while I was still here on leave. And now that it has really happened, I am grateful. And on the whole, gratitude that he was part of my life will always be greater than my grief at his no longer being here, physically here. I am at my desk; it is quiet in my room, and I shall sit for many hours yet in the light of my small lamp.

I am not going back to Westerbork tomorrow. All sorts of old aches and pains have turned up again in my body, and for the last two days I have been seeing a good doctor who has yet to finish his examination. I have to find out first what is the matter with me and then what to do about it. I shall need to develop quite a new kind of patience to deal with this unexpected situation.

And you will write to me, won't you?

That's all for now. Please give my regards to anyone you think would like to have them, especially Rosenberg.[5] And *auf Wiedersehen*, all right?

Etty

How glad my abandoned typewriter must have been to have something nice written on it again! To think that somewhere in Holland there is a heath with a small village of wooden barracks and that a man lives there called Osias Kormann, who has fine eyes behind his spectacles, and who writes to me, "You are truly creative, you have brought into being something around me that is alive"—I was really moved by that.

I am grateful to my stomach, which you must know "inside out" by now, for keeping me here a few weeks longer. I shall be fully composed when I return. If it's true that the transports have stopped, and that we shall be spending the winter cooped up with a lot of people, then there is a great moral task before us, don't you agree? The cold and the dark and the pea soup and the barbed wire are things we shall share out equitably among ourselves and perhaps even bear together. But "bearing" is a thing that has to be learned; the Dutch are not yet very good at it. And then there is the animosity between the German and the Dutch Jews, which is something we must fight against as hard as we can. All sorts of strange things will happen, and one day I imagine we'll have many tales to tell. I wish I were there. I have so much love in me, you know, for Germans and Dutchmen, Jews and non-Jews, for the whole of mankind—there is more than enough to go around.

If everything happens as it should, next Thursday a group of our people will come here on leave.[6] On the Wednesday after that, they will return to Westerbork, and I hope to go back with them.

One day when there is no more barbed wire left in the world, you must come and see my room. It is so beautiful and peaceful. I spend half my nights at my desk reading and writing by the light of my small lamp. I have about

1,500 pages of a diary from last year, and one of these days I shall read it through. What a rich life leaps out at me from every page! To think that it was my life—and still is. You really don't know very much about me, nor I about you. Facts, I mean. But facts don't really matter in life, only what you have become through them. So we do after all know a little bit about each other, I think. Don't you?

What else shall I tell you? There's nothing much. It is nine o'clock. Perhaps tonight for once I really shall go to bed early. It's very important to do that now and then, but it's always a gigantic struggle to tear myself away from this desk. You've got my books, I'm told. I'm glad about that.

Do you ever see my comrade-in-arms, Vleeschhouwer?[7]

So as not to write just about my desk, let me tell you that I spend two hours every day at the dentist's. I am sinking what family capital I have left into my holey teeth, so that when I come back I will be restored in more than just spirit.

And now, my friend, that's enough till we meet next time, whether on paper or face to face. Remember me particularly to Rosenberg—I often think of him.

All the best,
Etty

Oh yes, something I've always wanted to ask: when and where did you lose that little piece of your poor nice index finger? Was it very painful?

Oh Kormann, my Kormann,

It's getting so wet and cold here, I can't imagine what it must be like for you, what with the shortage of food and blankets. My heart has been so terribly heavy today thinking about you. But who knows? Perhaps that's got nothing to do with you; perhaps I'm sad and impatient because my recovery is so slow. How are you, then, my dear friend? Have you moved yet, and was it a lot of bother?

On one of our walks beside the yellow lupin fields, we spoke about wishes and their fulfillment. Do you remember? My poet, Rainer Maria Rilke, says something marvelous about it in one of his letters. Your colleague Haussmann would probably retort bitterly, "This is no time for poets and philosophers." I don't know if he's right. In any case, I have copied a few sentences for you; perhaps it'll give you pleasure in a quiet moment (if you ever have such a thing):

"I've often had cause to suppose that wishing somehow brings its own fulfillment. So long as one wishes feebly, the wish is half a thing and requires its other half, its fulfillment, to stand whole.

"It's a wonder, though, how wishes can mature into something rounded, replete, entire, something on which one can't improve and that inspires and shapes and feeds on itself alone.

"Occasionally it seems that the source of a great, intensely lived life must lie precisely in its having indulged in wishes that were too grand, that thrust deed after deed, effect upon effect into life like a compulsion from within. Lost to their original aim, and purely elemental now, like a rushing, falling stream, they were converted into action or affection, unmediated being or blithe courage, as events and opportunity dictated."

. . .

So that's all for today. Please give my regards to Dr. Petzal—I like him so much. His face, which I often call to mind, seems to carry a secret melancholy behind its ironic mask. He can't be having a very easy time in his overcrowded hut.

Nor, alas, can any of you.

I long to be back to find out how you are getting on.

I believe we can extract something positive from life under any circumstances. But we have the right to say that only if we do nothing to escape, even from the worst conditions. I often think we should shoulder our rucksacks, join the others, and go "on transport" with them—

Later I'll sing a different tune.

Auf Wiedersehen, my dear.

Etty

WESTERBORK

Monday, 1:00 p.m., in the Mahlers' cubbyhole, where Eichenwald is at this moment making me porridge.[8]

My dear people,[9]

I really am going to send off a letter to you at last. This is the fifth time I've started. One experiences too much here and goes about with too many conflicting feelings to be able to write. Anyway, I can't. So I just send you my greetings. Besides, I think I'm going to have to come back to Amsterdam fairly quickly to have myself finished off in a high-class abattoir. I'm no good for anything, it's really very sad, there is so much to be done here. But there it is, something inside me has gone wrong, I am living on painkillers and will probably turn up without warning under your dearly loved noses. There is nothing I can do about it. Funny, I've been here nearly three days—it could be three weeks. It isn't as "idyllic" as in the summer, nothing like. I'll go and have a nap, and after that I'll start the endless march again through the barracks and the mud. What a pity I can't stay; I wish so much that I could.

Vleeschhouwer is just coming in; I'll give him this letter. Goodbye for now, everyone, and please forgive this short, messy scribble.

Lots of love,
Etty

Father Han, Käthe, Hans, Sister Maria, greetings, that's all.

I find it impossible to write here, not for lack of time but because of all the different impressions that come bursting in. I'm sure I could talk for a year at a stretch about this one week. I am on the leave list for next Saturday. What a privilege to be able to get away from here and see you all again. I'm glad I didn't plunge into the thick of things during the first few days; once in a while I take to my bed for an hour, and then things are all right again. Suitcase, clothes, and blankets are ready. The Mahlers take wonderful care of me. It is now half past eight and I am sitting once more in their hospitable little nook, a real oasis. Next to me Vleeschhouwer is immersed in a book. Mahler and his wife and two friends are playing cards. Little Eichenwald, my faithful milk-provider, sits on the floor in a corner next to the dog Humpie, unpicking the seams of Mijnheer Speyer's coat, which he wants to turn into a lumber jacket. Sterzenbach's brother (this is for Hans) is writing letters and in a moment will tell us more about his prison experiences.[10] Auntie Leah's trusty little stove stands in the corner brewing all sorts of good things for the assembled company. Just now Witmondt came in (I visited his wife a few times in Amsterdam; the people around me are all such close friends that I feel you know them well too). He was wearing a voluminous cape and we shouted in chorus, "Good God, Max, how did you come by that magnificent cape?" And Max—who looked like a skeleton when he was brought here from Amersfoort and has been carefully nursed by the Mahlers—said solemnly and dramatically, "This cape is still covered with blood from Amersfoort"—and there *were* some dark red spots on it.

What a lurid story! I am sitting squashed into a corner, barely managing to write. Just now another young man came in, one from Kattenburg, who is due to go on transport in the morning. All this is happening in a little room measuring two meters by three.

The central heating is on—yes, really—and the men are sitting in their shirt sleeves. Everything here is full of paradox. In the big barracks, where so many people have to lie on metal springs without mattresses or blankets, they are dying of cold. In the little huts, where there is central heating, people can't sleep at night for the heat. I share one of these huts with five roommates. Two double bunks, so unsteady on their legs that when the fat Viennese woman above me turns over at night, the bed shakes like a ship in a storm. And mice nibble at our bedding and our food supplies, which can be somewhat disquieting.

And what do I actually do in this place? I'm back to juggling five miserable mugs to share out coffee among hundreds of people. Now and then I run away out of sheer frustration—like last time, when a little old woman fainted in a corner and there wasn't a single drop of water to be had in the whole camp, because the water supply had been cut off. And then the people from Ellecom came. They were taken straight to the hospital. I sat by their beds stupefied. I still can't get it into my head that people can do such things to each other, and that some live to tell the tale.

I have started a small campaign to bring the library, which is stored in the cellar of a locked warehouse, out into the light of day. Everyone recognizes the need for books, but nothing gets done for lack of space. On Tuesday I'm going to have a talk with Paul Cronheim,[11] the Wagner man, and with the notary Spier. I should so much like to help provide some spiritual nourishment; I'll see what chance there is of that.

It is certainly not very pretty here: a gypsy life, poverty, mud. This afternoon I went into a couple of the bigger barracks, where several children seemed to be dying before my eyes—

Dear children, I may not be writing with much inspiration, but I'm glad to be here. As for my health, I'm not completely fit yet. All sorts of little complaints haunt me, but never mind; I'll see to them later.

This is hardly a real letter, but I felt so guilty that I had sent you only one depressing little scrawl. Westerbork completely swallows me up. By the end of the week I'll have surfaced again. No, it is impossible to write from here; it would take the better part of a lifetime to digest it all. And how wonderful it will be to be with you again next week! Thanks for your letter, Papa Han. And lots and lots of love to all of you.

Till the weekend,
Etty

AMSTERDAM

This time, as usual, I came back with various commissions from the heath. An ex-soubrette with gallstones asked for some hair dye. Then there was a girl who couldn't get out of bed because she had no shoes. And all sorts of other trifles. Not that the lack of shoes is a trifle, of course. And there was the commission from Dr. K. that I undertook with great pleasure, but I find that it weighs more and more heavily on me. The soubrette has long since dyed her hair again and the girl-without-shoes is able to get out of her bed again and brave the mud, but I have still not been able to fulfill Dr. K.'s request. To be honest, that's not just because I haven't been well for a few weeks.

A few evenings before I left Westerbork, I went to his austere little office, where he sometimes sits working deep into the night. He looked tired and thin and pale. He pushed a thick file aside for a moment, after first telling me some remarkable things about it, with appropriate humor. Then he looked around as if searching for something and with some difficulty found a few words: He had been feeling like an old man the last few months. The war would be over one day, surely . . . To start with, he would probably want to go and sit for a long time deep in a large forest and forget a good deal . . . then he might want to go and see Seville and Málaga, for where he should have memories of these cities, there are just a couple of gaps. He would also like to go back to work . . . there would surely be a League of Nations . . . How we suddenly got from the League of Nations to the two sisters in the Hague, one fair and one dark, I no longer remember. But, he said, once I was back in Amsterdam on leave, could I possibly write to them, something in my style, about life in Westerbork?

"Yes," said I, with much understanding, "it is certainly important to keep in touch with the outside world."

Your friend K. said almost indignantly, "Outside world? These two women mean much more to us here than just the outside world; they mean a whole part of our lives." And then, in that bare little office on that late evening, he spoke so movingly about you both that I gladly agreed to his request. But to be frank: now, sitting down to write, I'm not sure what exactly to tell you about life in Westerbork.

It was summer when I came here for the first time. Up till then, all I'd known about Drenthe was that it had a lot of megalithic tombs. And then suddenly there was a village of wooden barracks, set between heath and sky, with a glaringly yellow lupin field in the middle and barbed wire all around. And there were human lives as well, thick as flies. To be honest, I had never realized that refugees from Germany had already been held on Drenthe heath for four years, years in which I had been busy taking up collections for Spanish and Chinese children.[13]

During the first few days I walked around as if through the pages of a history book. I met people who had been in Buchenwald and Dachau at a time when to us these were only distant, threatening sounds. I met people who traveled all around the world on that ship without being allowed to disembark at any port.[14] You must have heard of that; the papers were full of it. I have seen snapshots of little children who are probably now growing up in some unknown corner of this earth. Who knows whether they will even recognize their parents—if they ever see them again?

In short, one had the feeling of seeing in tangible form a small part of the Jewish predicament of the last ten years. And we had thought there was nothing at Drenthe except megalithic tombs. It was enough to take your breath away.

In the summer of 1942—it seems years ago; so much more has happened in a few months than can be told in a few pages—this small settlement was turned upside down and shaken to the marrow. With horror, the old camp inmates witnessed the mass deportation of Jews from Holland to eastern Europe. From the very beginning they had to make their own considerable contribution in terms of human lives when the quota of "voluntary workers" was not completely filled.

One summer evening I sat eating red cabbage at the edge of the yellow lupin field that stretched from our dining hut to the delousing station, and with sudden inspiration I said, "One ought to write a chronicle of Westerbork." An older man to my left—also eating red cabbage—answered, "Yes, but to do that you'd have to be a great poet."

He is right, it would take a great poet. Little journalistic pieces won't do. The whole of Europe is gradually being turned into one great prison camp. The whole of Europe will undergo this same bitter experience. To simply record the bare facts of families torn apart, of possessions plundered and liberties forfeited, would soon become monotonous. Nor is it possible to pen picturesque accounts of barbed wire and vegetable swill to show outsiders what it's like. Besides, I wonder how many outsiders will be left if history continues along the paths it has taken.

There you are—I could tell right away that nothing would come of my report on Westerbork. The first attempt has got me bogged down in generalities. On the whole, a person more or less contemplative by nature isn't really suited to describing a specific place or event. One discovers that the basic materials of life are the same everywhere, and that one can live one's life with meaning—or else one can die—in any spot on this earth. The Big Dipper looks down on some distant hamlet just as reliably as it does on a great city at the hub of a nation, or as it does on a coal mine in Silesia; so that all's right with the world . . .

All I really want to say is this: I am no poet. And I am rather at my wits' end to know how to honor my promise to K. For although the name Westerbork is highly charged for us, and will reverberate in our ears for the rest of our lives, I don't know precisely what I can say about it. Life there is so eventful, although many may consider it deadly boring.

But on the morning after I heard your friend K. speak the names of Seville and Málaga with such fanatical longing, I met him on the narrow paved path between barracks 14 and 15. He was wearing his usual trilby hat, which makes him seem so out of place among all the wooden planks and low doors. He was walking quickly because he was hungry, but he still found time when we passed to say pointedly, "Have you thought about what I asked you? You know, making the acquaintance of those two sisters will greatly enrich your life too."

And so I find myself at an unheard-of late hour facing a blank piece of paper after all.

Yes—Westerbork.

If I understand it correctly, this place, now a focus of Jewish suffering, lay deserted and empty just four years ago. And the spirit of the Department of Justice hovered over the heath.

"There wasn't a butterfly to be seen here, not a flower, not even a worm," the very first German inmates told me emphatically. And now? Let me give you a rough idea from the inventory. We have an orphanage, a synagogue, a small mortuary, and a shoe-repair factory under construction. I have heard talk of a madhouse being built, and my latest information is that the expanding hospital barracks complex already has a thousand beds.

The two-person jail that stands like something out of an operetta in one corner of the camp is apparently no longer large enough, for they plan to build a bigger one. It must sound strange to you: a prison within a prison.

There are minor "cabinet crises," what with all the people who like to have a finger in every pie.

We have a Dutch commandant and a German one. The first is taller, but the second has more of a say. We are told, moreover, that he likes music and that he is a gentleman. I'm no judge, although I must say that for a gentleman he certainly has a somewhat peculiar job.

There is a hall with a stage where, in the glorious past when the word "transport" had not yet been heard, a rather faltering Shakespeare production was once put on. At the moment people sit at typewriters on the same stage.

There is mud, so much mud that somewhere between your ribs you need to have a great deal of inner sunshine if you don't want to become the psychological victim of it all. The physical effects, such as broken shoes and wet feet, you will certainly understand.

Although the camp buildings are all one story, you can hear as many accents as if the Tower of Babel had been erected in our midst: Bavaria and Groningen, Saxony and Limburg, the Hague and East Friesland; you can hear German with a Polish accent and German with a Russian accent; you find all sorts of dialects from Holland and Berlin—all in an area of half a kilometer square.

The barbed wire is more a question of attitude.

"*Us* behind barbed wire?" an indestructible old gentleman once said with a melancholy wave of his hand. "*They* are the ones who live behind barbed wire"—and he pointed to the tall villas that stand like sentries on the other side of the fence.

If the barbed wire just encircled the camp, then at least you would know where you were. But these twentieth-century wires meander about inside the camp too, around the barracks and in between, in a labyrinthine and unfathomable network. Now and then you come across people with scratches on their faces or hands.

There are watchtowers at the four corners of our wooden village, each a windswept platform on four tall posts. A man with a helmet and a gun stands outlined against the changing skies. In the evening one sometimes hears a shot echo across the heath, as it did once when the blind man stumbled too close to the barbed wire.

Finding something to say about Westerbork is also difficult because of its ambiguous character. On the one hand it is a stable community in the making, a forced one to be sure, yet with all the characteristics of a human society. And on the other hand, it is a camp for a people in transit, great waves of human beings constantly washed in from the cities and provinces, from rest homes, prisons, and other prison camps, from all the nooks and crannies of the Netherlands—only to be deported a few days later to meet their unknown destiny.

You can imagine how dreadfully crowded it is in half a square kilometer. Naturally, few follow the example of the man who packed his rucksack and went on transport of his own accord. When asked why, he said that he wanted the freedom to decide to go when *he* wanted to go. It reminds me of the Roman judge who said to a martyr, "Do you know that I have the power to have you killed?" And the martyr answered, "Yes, but I have the power of letting myself be killed."

Anyway, it is terribly crowded in Westerbork, as when

too many drowning people cling to the last bit of flotsam after a ship has sunk. People would rather spend the winter behind barbed wire in Holland's poorest province than be dragged away to unknown parts and unknown destinies deep within Europe, from where only a few indistinct sounds have come back to the rest of us. But the quota must be filled; so must the train, which comes to fetch its load with mathematical regularity. You cannot keep everyone back as being indispensable to the camp, or too sick for transport, although you try it with a great many. You sometimes think it would be simpler to put yourself on transport than have to witness the fear and despair of the thousands upon thousands of men, women, children, infants, invalids, the feebleminded, the sick, and the aged, who pass through our helping hands in an almost uninterrupted flow.

My fountain pen cannot form words strong enough to convey even the remotest picture of these transports. From the outside the impression is of bleak monotony, yet every transport is different and has its own atmosphere.

When the first transport passed through our hands, there was a moment when I thought I would never again laugh and be happy, that I had changed suddenly into another, older person cut off from all former friends. But on walking through the crowded camp, I realized again that where there are people, there is life. Life in all its thousands of nuances—"with a smile and a tear," to put it in popular terms.

It made a great difference whether people arrived prepared, with well-filled rucksacks, or had been suddenly dragged out of their houses or swept up from the streets. In the end we saw only the last.

After the first of the police roundups, when people arrived in slippers and underclothes, the whole of Westerbork, in a single horrified and heroic gesture, stripped to

27

the skin. And we have tried, with the close cooperation of people on the outside, to make sure that those who leave are equipped as well as possible. But if we remember all those who went to face the winter in eastern Europe without any clothes, if we remember the single thin blanket that was sometimes all we were able to dole out in the night, a few hours before departure . . .

The slum-dwellers arrived from the cities, displaying their poverty and neglect in the bare barracks. Aghast, many of us asked ourselves: what sort of democracy did we really have?

The people from Rotterdam were in a class by themselves, hardened by the bombing raids. "We don't frighten easily anymore," you often heard them say. "If we survived all that, we'll survive this too." And a few days later they marched singing to the train. But it was midsummer then, and there were no old people yet, or invalids on stretchers bringing up the rear . . .

The Jews from Heerlen and Maastricht and thereabouts came telling stories that reverberated with the great send-off the province of Limburg had given them.[15] One felt that morally they could live on it for a long time. "The Catholics have promised to pray for us, and they're better at that than we are!" said one of them.

People came with all their rivalries. The Jews from Haarlem said somewhat loftily and acidly: "Those Amsterdammers have a grim sense of humor."

There were children who would not accept a sandwich before their parents had had one. There was a remarkable day when the Jewish Catholics or Catholic Jews—whichever you want to call them—arrived, nuns and priests wearing the yellow star on their habits.[16] I remember two young novices, twins, with identical beautiful, dark ghetto faces and serene, childish eyes peering out from under their skullcaps. They said with mild surprise that they had been fetched at half-past four from morning mass, and that they had eaten red cabbage in Amersfoort.

There was a priest, still fairly young, who had not left his monastery for fifteen years. He was out in the "world" for the first time, and I stood next to him for a while, following his eyes as they wandered peacefully around the barracks where the newcomers were being received.

The others—shaven, beaten, maltreated—who poured in along with the Catholics that day stumbled about the wooden hut with movements that were still unsteady and stretched out their hands toward the bread, of which there was not enough.

A young Jew stood very still next to us. His jacket was much too loose, but a grin broke through his stubbly black beard when he said, "They tried to smash the wall of the prison with my head, but my head was harder than the wall!"

Among all the shaved heads, it was strange to see the white-turbaned women who had just been treated in the delousing barracks, and who went about now looking distressed and humiliated.

Children dozed off on the dusty plank floor; others played tag among the adults. Two little ones floundered helplessly around the heavy body of a woman lying unconscious in a corner. They didn't understand why their mother just lay there without answering them. A gray-haired old gentleman, straight as an arrow and with a clear-cut, aristocratic profile, stared at the whole infernal canvas and repeated over and over to himself: "A terrible day! A terrible day!"

And among all this, the unremitting clatter of a battery of typewriters: the machine-gun fire of bureaucracy.

Through the many little windowpanes one can see other wooden barracks, barbed wire, and a blasted heath.

I looked at the priest who was now back in the world

29

again. "And what do you think of the world now?" I asked. But his gaze remained unwavering and friendly above the brown habit, as if everything he saw was known, familiar from long ago. That same evening, a man later told me, he saw some priests walking one behind the other in the dusk between two dark barracks. They were saying their rosaries as imperturbably as if they had just finished vespers at the monastery. And isn't it true that one can pray anywhere, in a wooden barracks just as well as in a stone monastery, or indeed, anywhere on this earth where God, in these troubled times, feels like casting his likeness?

For those who have been granted the nerve-shattering privilege of being allowed to stay in Westerbork "until further notice," there is the great moral danger of becoming blunted and hardened.

The human suffering that we have seen during the last six months, and still see daily, is more than anyone can be expected to comprehend in half a year. No wonder we hear on all sides every day, in every pitch of voice, "We don't want to think, we don't want to feel, we want to forget as soon as possible." It seems to me that this is a very great danger.

True, things happen here that in the past our reason would not have judged possible. But perhaps we have faculties other than reason in us, faculties that in the past we didn't know we had but that possess the ability to grapple with the incomprehensible. I believe that for every event, man has a faculty that helps him deal with it.

If we were to save only our bodies and nothing more from the camps all over the world, that would not be enough. What matters is not whether we preserve our lives at any cost, but *how* we preserve them. I sometimes think that every new situation, good or bad, can enrich us with new insights. But if we abandon the hard facts that we are forced to face, if we give them no shelter in our heads and hearts, do not allow them to settle and change into impulses through which we can grow and from which we can draw meaning—then we are not a viable generation. It is not easy—and no doubt less easy for us Jews than for anyone else—yet if we have nothing to offer a desolate postwar world but our bodies saved at any cost, if we fail to draw new meaning from the deep wells of our distress and despair, then it will not be enough. New thoughts will have to radiate outward from the camps themselves, new insights, spreading lucidity, will have to cross the barbed wire enclosing us and join with the insights that people outside will have to earn just as bloodily, in circumstances that are slowly becoming almost as difficult. And perhaps, on the common basis of an honest search for some way to understand these dark events, wrecked lives may yet take a tentative step forward.

That's why it seemed such a great danger to me when all around one could hear, "We don't want to think, we don't want to feel, it's best to shut your eyes to all this misery." As if suffering—in whatever form and however it may come to us—were not also part of human existence.

I see that I have strayed far beyond your friend K.'s innocuous request. After all, I was to tell you something about life in Westerbork, not about my own views. I couldn't help it, they just slipped out.

But what about the old people? All those aged, infirm people? What use is my philosophy when I have to face them? In the history of Westerbork, surely the saddest chapter will be the one that deals with the old. Probably even sadder than the story of the people from Ellecom, who arrived mutilated, sending a shudder of horror throughout the camp.

To the young and healthy, you can say something that you believe in and can act upon in your own life: that history has indeed laid a heavy destiny on our shoulders, and that we must try and attain the grandeur we need to bear it. You can even say that we should consider ourselves front-line soldiers, although we are sent to very peculiar fronts. It may seem as if we are doomed to complete passivity, but no one can prevent us from mobilizing our inner forces. No one. But have you ever heard of front-line soldiers aged eighty, bearing the red-and-white canes of the blind as their weapons?

One summer morning I came upon a man mumbling to himself, "For heaven's sake, look at the kind of labor forces for Germany they've sent us now!" And when I hurried around to the entrance, masses of old people were just being unloaded from dilapidated trucks onto our heath. There we stood, almost beyond speech. That was really going too far, we thought. But later on we knew better and would ask each other with every new transport: "And— how many old people and invalids this time?"

There was a little old woman who had left her spectacles and her medicine bottle at home on the mantel—could she go and get them now, and where exactly was she, and where would she be going?

A woman of eighty-seven clung to my hand with so much strength that I thought she would never let go. She told me how the steps in front of her little house had always gleamed and how she had never in her life thrown her clothes under the bed when she went to sleep.

And the bowed little gentleman of seventy-nine: he had been married for more than fifty years, he told me; his wife was in the hospital in Utrecht and he was about to be taken out of Holland the next day . . .

Even if I went on for pages, I still couldn't convey any idea of the shuffling and the stumbling and the falling down, the need for help along with the childish questions. You can't do much with words. A helping hand on the shoulder is sometimes too heavy. Oh no, these old people, they need a chapter to themselves. Their helpless gestures and exhausted faces crowd many a sleepless night . . .

In a few months the population has swelled from a thousand to roughly ten thousand. The greatest influx dates from the awful days of October, when after a massive Jew hunt throughout the Netherlands, Westerbork was swept by a human flood that threatened to engulf it.

Hence this is not exactly an organically evolved community, with its own even rhythms. Yet—and this is what takes the breath away—you can find every attitude here, every class, ism, conflict, and current of society. And the area still remains only half a kilometer square.

In retrospect is that really so surprising, since every individual carries deep in his inner being the trend, the part of society, the cultural level he represents? But what always strikes one anew is that even at a time of shared distress these distinctions are maintained.

One day in the mud between two big barracks I met a girl who told me she had ended up in Westerbork by chance. This is a typical phenomenon: everyone views his *own* case as an unfortunate accident. We have not yet gained a common sense of history. But to come back to the girl: she told me a pathetic tale of little packages that failed to arrive and of a pair of lost shoes. And then her face brightened and she said: "But we have been lucky with people; our barracks is full of the best people. Do you know what they call it? The bocht van de Herengracht!"[17] Confounded, I looked from her worn-out shoes to her made-up face and did not know whether to laugh or cry.

Of all the shortages in Westerbork concentration camp, the shortage of space is surely the worst.

About two and a half thousand of the more than ten thousand people are housed in two hundred and fifteen small huts, which used to be the main part of the camp and which held one family each in pretransport times.

Every little hut has two small rooms, sometimes three, and a little kitchen with a faucet and a WC. There is no doorbell, which makes entering a quick and unceremonious business. As soon as you open the front door, you're standing in the middle of the kitchen. If you're there to visit friends who live in the little back room, then with your newly acquired informality you rush straight through the front room, where another family may be sitting at the table or having a fight or getting ready for bed. And for some time now, these little rooms have usually been crammed with visitors eager to escape for a while from the big barracks. The hut dwellers are housed like princes by comparison, envied and constantly besieged by all Westerbork.

The scandalous shortage of space in Westerbork is really clear in the colossal, hastily built barracks, those jampacked hangars of drafty slats where, under a lowering sky made up of hundreds of people's drying laundry, the iron bunks are stacked in triple decks.

The poor French would never have suspected that Jews, exiled to one Drenthe heath or another, would someday dream their fearful dreams on beds built for the Maginot Line. I'm told that's where these bunks come from.

On these iron beds people live and die, eat, fall ill, or lie awake through the night, because so many children cry, or because they cannot help wondering why so little news comes from the thousands who have already set out from this place.

The beds provide the only storage space there is: suitcases lie under them and rucksacks hang over the iron bars. The other furniture consists of rough wooden tables and narrow wooden benches. Matters of hygiene I shall not mention in this modest account, lest I cause you some unappetizing moments.

Scattered through this vast space are a few stoves, which don't even give enough heat for the old ladies crowded around them. How people are expected to live through the winter in these barracks has not yet been made clear.

All these great human warehouses have been put up in precisely the same manner in the middle of the mud and have been furnished in the same, let us say austere, style. But the remarkable thing is that while a trip through one barracks may make you feel you are in a squalid slum, another will give the impression of a solid middle-class district. In fact, every bunk and every rough wooden table seems to radiate its own atmosphere.

I know of a table in one of the barracks where a candle burns in a glass lantern every evening. Some eight people usually sit around it, and it's called the "bohemian corner." When you go on a few steps to the next table, also with eight people sitting around it, the only difference may be that it holds a couple of dirty pans instead of a candle, but it is an entirely different world.

Like circumstances do not yet seem to produce like people.

Leading lights from cultural and political circles in the big cities have also been stranded on this barren stretch of heath five hundred by six hundred meters. With one mighty convulsion all their scenery has collapsed about them, and now they stand around a little hesitantly and awkwardly on this drafty, open stage called Westerbork.

These figures wrenched from their context still carry with them the restless atmosphere of a society more complicated than the one we have here. They walk along the thin barbed-wire fence. Their silhouettes move, life-sized and exposed, across the great stretch of sky. You cannot imagine it ... Their armor of position, esteem, and property has collapsed, and now they stand in the last shreds of their humanity. They exist in an empty space, bounded by earth and sky, which they must fill with whatever they can find within them—there is nothing else.

One suddenly realizes that it is not enough to be an able politician or a talented artist. In the most extreme distress, life demands quite other things.

Yes, it is true, our ultimate human values are being put to the test.

Perhaps I have persuaded you, with my chatter, that I have now told you something about Westerbork. But when I let Westerbork rise up in my mind's eye, in all its facets and with all its spiritual and material needs, I can see that success has eluded me. Furthermore, this is a very one-sided story. I could have told quite another, filled with hatred and bitterness and rebellion.

But rebellion born only when distress begins to affect one personally is no real rebellion and can never bear fruit. And the absence of hatred in no way implies the absence of moral indignation.

I know that those who hate have good reason to do so. But why should we always have to choose the cheapest and easiest way? It has been brought home to me here forcibly how every atom of hatred added to the world makes it an even more inhospitable place. And I also believe, childishly perhaps but stubbornly, that the earth will become more habitable again only through the love that the Jew Paul described to the citizens of Corinth in the thirteenth chapter of his first letter.

Saturday afternoon, 26 December [1942]

The more I think about it, the worse it seems that I have left you without news for so long. I wanted to write as soon as I got back here, to you and to Rosenberg and Haussmann: you were always so kind and hospitable, I felt so much at home with you. Haussmann's potato soup certainly lives as a culinary high point in my memory, and the Hanukkah lights in the big barracks are an even more precious memory because I was there with you.[18]

The reason I haven't managed to write is probably that I felt rather ill, quite apart from being downcast when the doctor told me I would have to rest for another five weeks. But my good humor is gradually creeping back.

I am so glad that I spent those weeks in Westerbork and that among other things I know how and where you live. Dear Osias, I promise that there won't be any more long pauses from now on. Please remember me to Rosenberg of course, and to your comrades Haussmann ("niece" and all) and Frank and Grüneberg, won't you? And lots and lots of love to you, from

Etty

Now look, Osias, this is terrible: have you really not received any letters at all from me up to now? That's the impression Vleeschhouwer gave me. How treacherous you must think I am! But I must be honest and confess: I have written you only once so far, though at some length, in the middle of the night, with a promise to write again soon. But the "soon" stretched into a few weeks.

You know, Osias, I have many friends. Some come to me with their spiritual needs, and those I must talk to for a long time. Then there are others to whom I write regularly and in detail because I know that they need it and also because I want to help them. But with you it's quite different: you are there in my life, your absence from it is unimaginable. I often have conversations with you, but feel no need to write them down; I always believe you'll sense them without letters. So if you don't hear from me for some time you mustn't be disappointed or even unhappy; I still have the same strong, good feelings about you. This morning as I lay thinking of you, I was suddenly overwhelmed with the need to tell you again that I should be terribly sorry if you thought I cared less for you than before. Everything decent and beautiful that I have shared with you has become part of my emotional life, and will always be there.

I hope my first letter has arrived by now. There were a few bits and pieces in it I very much wanted you to see. Are you very busy? Would it be possible sometime to have a few words from you? And are you still living with good old Rosenberg in the quiet back room? How I would love to be fit again and surprise you by just turning up. Meanwhile my orders are: rest, rest, and more rest. But even in bed one can live one's life, or at least try to.

Until another time, Osias Kormann!

In friendship,
Etty

Regards to Rosenberg.

Greetings from a girl with an excruciating big toe, Osias. You may recall that this girl is a good friend of yours or you may have forgotten, since so much goes on where you are—too much.

As for me, the same contradiction still applies: the spirit is livelier and more creative than ever, but the flesh cannot form a structure solid enough to support so ardent a spirit.

However, I am patient—not always, of course—and live sensibly so as to be well again as soon as possible. And then I'll turn up again. You must have some work for me by now in the. "V," or are there already too many people and not enough room?[19]

Your village has been suddenly turned into a city, without doubt a very sad and strange one.

I have the uneasy suspicion that you don't sleep at all anymore. You ought to now and then. You will, won't you please?

So Rosenberg's mother has arrived. How is he coping? Is he able to make her life a little easier? My very best wishes to them, please. And to Unger as well.

These days many people think: life is coming to an end, this is a great eclipse. Perhaps much later it will be seen as a new beginning as well. Why don't I keep my feet on the ground? Am I a dreamer? Oh please let me be, there have to be people like me, too. My realities may be different from what most people call reality, but still they *are* realities.

Osias Kormann, dear friend on the Drenthe heath— what a bizarre business life really is—I send you my love, I'm very fond of you.

Etty

Is it a long time since I last wrote you, Osias? It feels like just a few days, but that goes to show how quickly time passes for me.

Anyway, may I smile on you again from afar? I have a doctor who gets furious when I come into his office beaming. He says it's unforgivable to smile at all in times like these. I think he's wrong; what do you say? Hello, Osias, how are you, what are you up to? Are you very busy?[20] Are you in a good mood? Will you need an assistant in the near future? I don't ask for high wages, just friendly treatment. For now I am still going in for morning exercises, the sun, the Bible, Russian, potato-peeling, literature, and conversations with much-too-optimistic or much-too-pessimistic, polemical, suicidal, angry, sad, or what-have-you people. A varied program, you can see. And for the rest, I still have a young heart and old bones; the balance between them could be a bit better. My doctor is unable to come up with anything wiser at the moment. He says that most people in these unbearable times suffer in the soul and the mind, but with me the sufferer is the body. Though I swallow bitter, sweet, sour, solid, and liquid things in turn, I'm sure it's a lot of nonsense and we should look to nature for restoration. All in all, however, I think I will be a useful person again one day, and you'll make fabulous coffee when I come back, won't you?

Lots of love, Osias, and think kindly now and then of

Etty

And best wishes to Rosenberg.

It seems that the good Lord and the *Zentralstelle*[21] don't want me to have coffee with you this week; we shall have to wait and see whether next week brings my travel permit. I hope you are especially well in all respects, my dear Osias; it would be nice if I could come and see for myself.

How are the yellow lupins—are they out again? And are you having spring now and then, despite everything? And give my regards to Rosenberg. And accept a harmless but nonetheless heartfelt hug from

Etty

Until next week, then. And regards from my father, who was glad to receive your greetings. And don't spoil your nice eyes, please, with these awful hieroglyphics. (I used to write everything on the typewriter, but lately I've had to get used to writing by hand again.)

'Bye,
E.

My watch has broken, Osias. Now I absolutely must come back to Westerbork, since there isn't a single person left in Amsterdam with time to mend a watch. You know that my needs are few, but one thing I cannot do without is a watch. As you can probably guess, there are a few other reasons, too, why I want to be back among you all. And I look forward to seeing you yourself just a tiny bit!

I have more glad tidings, especially for you: my wisdom tooth has emerged, not without severe labor pains, but in the end it proved to be there. So you can still entertain hopes that I will be wise one day. What does wise mean to you: egoistic? All this egoism is getting so boring. Since people have been telling each other for centuries that man is basically an egoist, one begins to believe it and actually becomes egoistic. There are so many sides to a human being that it would be nice to try something else, just for a change from boring and unproductive egoism. Anyhow, we'll argue about that when we see each other, won't we? Your letter was nice; you're an old cynic but a very dear person.

In Westerbork I'll have to look out for hundreds of people—not only friends but the children, the parents, and the grandparents of friends. That will be a labor in itself, and other labor will surely turn up without my looking for it.

My dear friend, I look forward to seeing you—but I've said that already.

Until next week.

'Bye!
Etty

Osias my dear,

Again it must look as if I've been faithless but the real reason why I haven't written is just human inertia. Your coffee must have grown cold by now, but it's not my fault. I feel almost like a soldier awaiting his next orders. On the one hand I am grateful for every day I can spend here at my desk immersed in things that are close to me. On the other, I want nothing more than to be back with you all as soon as possible. When I stop to add it up, I see that I have already been away from your Heath Metropolis for five months, though oddly it feels like only a week—rather, it feels as if I've never been away at all. One could go on living in several places at once this way, couldn't one?

Osias, you know the Skating Club, next to the Concertgebouw? I sometimes go walking there with you along the railings, and we have such a lovely time together. Usually you arrive quite out of the blue. I take my customary turn around the club grounds, and suddenly you are at my side, and I delight in your closeness all over again.

As far as my health goes, I don't have much to complain about. I have admittedly become a shade less productive than I was before my illness, but that must be true of many people in this blessed Europe of ours.

Osias my dear, this must be enough for today. I am waiting anxiously to find out when we will see each other again at last—

Please give my special regards to Petzal. I mean so often to write to him, but—laziness, etc., as you well know. And best wishes again, of course, to Rosenberg.

And to yourself: most definitely *auf Wiedersehen!*

'Bye!
Etty

Friday afternoon, 21 May [1943]

My dear Osias,

Every evening for the past few days I have meant to send you another bulletin, but each day is so unsettled now. My blankets will have to wait up on your wooden gallery a little longer than I thought, until they can cover me again.

On the morning of April twenty-fourth my call-up came: I was to report on the twenty-fifth. I started getting my rucksack ready right away, but was told in the afternoon that my call-up had been an "error." That seems a curious expression, as if it wasn't an "error" for everyone else. Oh well, I shan't start philosophizing on this unpleasant subject now; we can talk to each other soon enough.

Today I heard that fifteen colleagues from the Jewish Council in Westerbork will get leave and fifteen volunteers here will be needed as replacements. I shall volunteer, of course, and then just wait and see whether they can use me, since I represent a somewhat peculiar, nihilistic faction. But I think we shall soon see each other in any case now that the "liquidation" of "Jewish remnants" has taken on a faster tempo.

To think that ten months have already passed since I met a small man with a gray cap and heavy spectacles in the school in Westerbork, and since that man told me fantastic stories about the camp and said afterwards, "You are definitely no Dutchwoman; you have too much warmth." Yes, Osias, and all the rest.

This is not really a letter, only a hasty greeting. I expect your work is sad again right now. *Auf Wiedersehen,* in a few days or in a few weeks, but anyway *auf Wiedersehen!*

Etty

[Note apparently left in Amsterdam]

Saturday evening, 5 June 1943

Little Maria,

Don't let's be too materialistic: a few days more or less, and whether or not we managed to see each other doesn't really matter to us, does it? It's a pity, I would so much have liked to see you, but that will happen again, I'm absolutely certain.

It is late; I can't tell you how tired I am. I had hoped to reach you by telephone in Wageningen, because I stayed a day longer, but I didn't manage it.

You ask for a diary. Because it's you, I'm leaving a silly piece of writing behind. There's a lot of rubbish in it, indiscreet woman that I am!

If you ever have a hard time, pour your soul out on a scrap of paper and send it to Etty; she'll be sure to answer you.

Look after Father Han—but you do that anyway. He'll tell you all sorts of thrilling stories about the last two days. I can hardly keep my eyes open; what hard work carrying a rucksack is! I am not saying good-bye; we are not really leaving each other, are we?

May all go very well with you, dear child.

Etty

WESTERBORK

AMSTERDAM

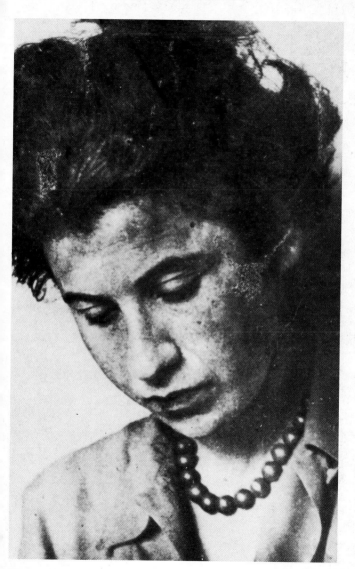

Etty Hillesum, about 1941

'One day when there is no more barbed wire left in the world, you must come and see my room. It is so beautiful and peaceful. I spend half my night at my desk reading and writing by the light of my small lamp. I have about 1,500 pages of a diary from last year, and one of these days I shall read it through. What a rich life leaps out at me from every page. To think that it was my life – and still is' (28 September 1942)

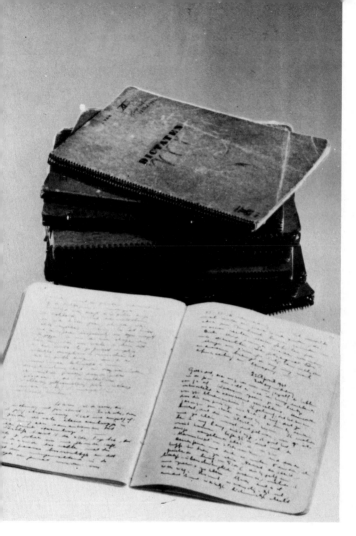

Eight exercise books closely written in a small hard-to-decipher
hand: the diaries of Etty Hillesum

ABOVE LEFT: Etty's mother, Rebecca Hillesum
ABOVE RIGHT: Etty's father, Dr Louis Hillesum, headmaster of Deventer Gymnasium
LEFT: Mischa Hillesum, the older of Etty's two brothers, a musical prodigy, one of Holland's best pianists
OPPOSITE ABOVE: Maria Tuinzing in her room, about 1939
OPPOSITE LEFT: Han Wegerif ('Father Han'), 1943
OPPOSITE RIGHT: 'The man who is closest to me': Julius Spier, reading hands

ABOVE LEFT: Johanna ('Jopie')
Smelik
ABOVE RIGHT: Christine van
Nooten
LEFT: Milli Ortmann

OPPOSITE PAGE
ABOVE LEFT: Klaas Smelik, Sr
ABOVE RIGHT: Henny ('Tide')
Tidemann
BELOW LEFT: Werner Levie,
director of the Jewish Theater
BELOW RIGHT: Liesl Levie,
Etty's best friend, now living in
Israel

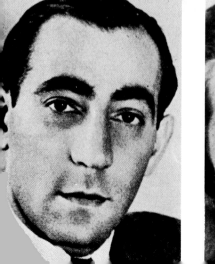

Roundup: the Jews summoned for Westerbork gather in Amsterdam-South

WESTERBORK

'A village of wooden barracks, set between heath and sky, a
glaringly yellow lupin field in the middle and barbed wire all
around.'

LEFT: Osias Kormann in Westerbork: 'dear friend on the Drenthe heath.'

RIGHT: Philip Mechanicus, author of *In Depôt,* a memoir of Westerbork. He told Etty: 'If I survive this time, I shall emerge a more mature and deeper person, and if I die, then I shall die a more mature and deeper one.'

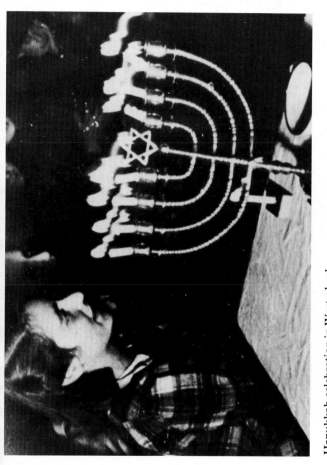

Hanukkah celebration in Westerbork

Administration barracks in Westerbork. At night, the place was used as a theater

OPPOSITE ABOVE: One of the 107 barracks in Westerbork: 'those jam-packed hangars of drafty slats where, under a lowering sky made up of hundreds of people's drying laundry, the iron bunks are stacked in triple decks' (December 1942)
OPPOSITE BELOW: Fifty yards away, Commandant A K Gemmeker's private quarters

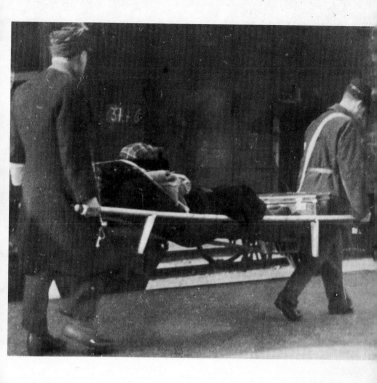

'Slowly but surely six o'clock in the morning has arrived. The train is due to depart at eleven, and they are starting to load it with people and luggage . . . The camp has been cut in two halves since yesterday by the train: a depressing series of bare, unpainted freight cars in the front, and a proper coach for the guards at the back. Some of the cars have paper mattresses on the floor. These are for the sick' (24 August 1943)

'We left the camp singing . . .' Etty's last postcard, thrown from the train; it was found and mailed on 15 September 1943

My very dear people,

Did you go on waving to my two rosebuds for a long time? You are all so dear to me; I held onto that thought during the whole train trip, and now the camp with its large-scale misery of transports coming and going has swallowed me whole again. I have been here a hundred years already. The journey was pleasant enough. There is a nice spirit of comradeship among our people. They told me some tall tales, starting with the news that we had to walk the whole way from Assen to the camp, luggage and all. I wasn't too pleased to hear that. But when they announced that a shop selling nougat had opened in the camp, that the orphanage had held a flower show, and that polo was the latest craze, my eyes were opened.

In Assen it was pouring rain and a leaky truck was waiting for us. We all were a bit wet when we arrived. Together with our dripping luggage we were ushered into a hall (which isn't what used to happen), where our rucksacks and suitcases were searched by the police. I readily opened the little bag with the Koran and the Talmud in it; they didn't bother with my rucksack, which is as big as a house, and I certainly didn't mind.

The hut where I have been put this time is something between a small storehouse and a boudoir. Beds, two or three tiers high, suitcases and boxes everywhere, flowers on the table and in the window, and a couple of languid females in long silk peignoirs. Most astonishing. I share my place with a former beauty queen from Het Leven.[22] At ten o'clock she propped a mirror against my butter dish and busied herself for half an hour with her eyebrows. There was no bed for me; but we had to work anyhow that night, because a transport from Vught had arrived. We were due to report at four a.m., so at eleven I rolled myself in a blanket, clothes and all (the sleeping bag was wet and had been hung up to dry), on a bed whose regular occupant was said to be working through the night. When I had been lying down for an hour, greatly enjoying the musical gnawings of the mice (which seem to have multiplied since I was last here), along came the bed's real tenant, a near-sighted lady with a pitch-black moustache from Lijnbaansgracht, a place I have never much liked. So then we lay side by side together on her narrow bunk—what you might call a piquant situation.

I woke up fairly stiff at about four o'clock. I fortified myself with your delicious wheaten creation, darling Käthe, and then walked again through the nocturnal Westerbork landscape. First of all we underwent a Lysol treatment, because so many lice always arrive from Vught. From four to nine I dragged screaming children around and carried luggage for exhausted women. It was hard going, and heart-rending. Women with small children, 1,600 (tonight another 1,600 will arrive); the men had been deliberately kept back in Vught. The morning transport is ready, Jopie and I have just been walking along it. Large, empty cattle cars. In Vught two or three children die every day. An old woman asked me helplessly, "Could you tell me, please could you tell me, why we Jews have to suffer so much?" I couldn't answer. There was a woman who had had to feed her four-month-old child on cabbage soup for days. She said, "I keep calling, 'Oh God, oh God'—but does He really still exist?" Among the prisoners I met an ex-assistant of Professor Scholten, who taught me procedural law once upon a time. I hardly recognized him because of his emaciation, beard, and staring eyes. I also met my internist, Schaap. When I was in the NIZ,[23] Schaap stood by my bed wearing an expression that implied my nonexistence and explained to the other doctors gathered around:

50

"Here lies a young lady who positively wants to go back to Westerbork," as if I were an incomprehensible case. Now he looked fit and cheerful (he has already been here for some time). This evening's delivery from Vught included his wife and children, who also looked quite good (tell Tide this[24]). On my journey through the camp this morning I met many old friends—friends of my parents, too. People whom I used to know as decent citizens, living in peaceful and comfortable circumstances, I now find inhabiting the big barracks as regular members of the proletariat. It is very moving, the state some of them are in. I'd rather not have my parents here. At the moment I am sitting in Jopie's little house and he is sitting opposite me in soldier's trousers and a dirty gray jacket. He sends you his kind regards. One of his best friends died a few hours ago. The friend's wife and child were sent through some time past; the man was in an advanced stage of TB and couldn't go with them. Jopie told me that theirs was one of the few good marriages he had known. Several days ago another good friend of his died.

This afternoon I shall try and get a little sleep; I now have a bed—someone went on leave today. At four in the morning another transport comes from Vught. Last night I was able to piece together a picture of Vught, a truly horrible picture.

I am glad I've come back to Westerbork. I am greeted warmly on all sides. I went to see Hedwig Mahler, who is being allowed to stay here for the time being, and met a woman who was once the headmistress at Father's school.[25] They gave me a bowl of semolina. Then I went to see Kormann, who almost killed me with pleasure and gave me another bowl of semolina. Later I went to visit someone else and was given more semolina. I let the rest of them have the cabbage. One and all seem to be well.

With everything I've been doing, it is now half-past

twelve. I have just fetched my bread ration and ten grams of butter from the kitchen, as well as a small vitamin C tablet, which was a surprise. Now I'll stop this muddled tale. Tonight at seven I'll go and see Herman B. in the hospital; I couldn't make it last night.[26] I can't do the night work the way I used to; I collapse in the middle. But don't worry—I'm not rushing at things headlong anymore. At the moment I itch all over despite the Lysol.

A hasty farewell to you all, too many to mention by name. You are all of you so very dear to me.

More later, dear people.
Etty

My little Maria,

Why don't you write Etty to say how you are? Are you happy, are you sad, do you rush around, do you sit quietly at home, what does Ernst have to say, what does Amsterdam have to say, what does Father Han do, does Käthe go to bed on time? As I walk through the mud between the wooden barracks, I feel as if I am walking at the same time along the corridors of my six-year home, or sitting at a shaky table in the noisy little parlor, or working at my beloved, untidy desk. I talk to many people here who say, "We don't want to remember anything from before; otherwise we couldn't manage to live here." But I can live here as well as I do just *because* I remember everything from "before" (it's not really a "before" for me), and I go on living.

Noon

My soul is content, Maria. I was given four hospital barracks today, one large and three small; I have to check whether the people there need any food or luggage from the outside. The wonderful thing about it is that I now have free access to the whole complex of hospital barracks at almost any time of day.

Later

Take these few words just as they come, little one. There isn't much time for writing here—but the letters I send you in my thoughts are much longer.

I am fine, and content. I live just as I did in Amsterdam, really; sometimes I don't even notice that I'm in a camp, which is very strange. And all of you are so close to me that I don't even miss you. Jopie is a cherished companion. In the evenings we go and watch the sun setting over the purple lupins behind the barbed wire. And if I get leave I'll probably be back.

Do write.

'Bye!
Etty

My dear people,

Not much heath is left now inside the barbed wire; more
barracks are always being added. Only a little piece remains in the furthest corner of the camp, and that's where
I'm sitting now, in the sun under a glorious blue sky,
among some low shrubbery. Right across from me only a
few meters away, a blue uniform with a helmet stands in
the watchtower. A guard with an enraptured expression is
picking purple lupins, his gun dangling on his back. When
I look to the left I see billowing white smoke and hear the
puffing of a locomotive. The people have already been
loaded onto the freight cars; the doors are closed. There
are many green police,[27] who sang this morning as they
marched by the side of the train, and the Dutch military
police are out as well. The quota of people who must go is
not yet filled. Just now I met the matron of the orphanage,
carrying a small child in her arms who also has to go,
alone. And a number of people have been taken out of the
hospital barracks. They are doing a thorough job here today; big shots from the Hague have come on a visit. It's
very strange watching these gentlemen at work from close
quarters. I've been up since four this morning dealing with
the babies and carrying luggage. In a few hours you can
accumulate enough gloom here to last a lifetime. The
nature-loving policeman has gathered his purple bouquet
now, perhaps he's off to court some farmer's daughter in
the neighborhood. The engine gives a piercing shriek. The
whole camp holds its breath; another three thousand Jews
are about to leave. There are babies with pneumonia lying
in the freight cars. Sometimes what goes on here seems
totally unreal. I haven't been given any particular job,
which suits me very well. I just wander about and find my

own work. This morning I had a brief talk with a woman who had come from Vught, who told me her latest experiences in three minutes. How much can you really tell in a few minutes? When we came to a door, and I wasn't allowed to go any further, she embraced me and said: "Thank you for being such a help."

Just now I climbed up on a box lying among the bushes here to count the freight cars. There were thirty-five, with some second-class cars at the front for the escorts. The freight cars had been completely sealed, but a plank had been left out here and there, and people put their hands through the gaps and waved as if they were drowning.

The sky is full of birds, the purple lupins stand up so regally and peacefully, two little old women have sat down on the box for a chat, the sun is shining on my face—and right before our eyes, mass murder. The whole thing is simply beyond comprehension.

Love
Etty

Dear Milli,[28]

Later on I'll write you a longer letter about this, the hardest day of my life. My parents and Mischa are being tremendous; I am amazed. The jam-packed freight train drew into the camp this morning. I stood beside it in the rain. The cars were shut tight, but there were a few small openings here and there high up, where the planks had been broken. Through one of these I suddenly spotted Mother's hat and Father's glasses and Mischa's peaky face. I started to shout and they saw me.

Now I shall have to share the same torture with them that I went through last night with the Levies and the two small children: registration, hours and hours of waiting, more registration outside in the rain, quarantine. Thanks to the many friends I have here, it'll be possible to make life easier for them in all sorts of small ways. Soon I'll have to take them to the large barracks, where all hell has been let loose. I don't think there are even enough beds for everyone, and there are no mattresses for the men. Still, my threesome is remarkably fit and cheerful and good-humored.

Now down to business. The Jewish Council thinks it imperative that you pursue the Barneveld option strenuously with the *Zentralstelle* on behalf of Mischa and the family (remember: not me!), and urges you to do so.[29] Perhaps you will still be able to get Mengelberg to intervene personally with Rauter.

Suddenly it's all coming to an end.

Etty

Christine,[30]

They are so indescribably efficient in this utter hell. In the early morning a line of freight cars pulled into the muddy camp. As I stood next to them I spotted my father's crumpled hat and glasses, my mother's hat, and Mischa's narrow face in a small opening high in one of the cars. And now that I am sharing their martyrdom, I am thankful I can take care of all sorts of minor details for them. Although at the moment there is nothing to take care of: what we have now is a complete catastrophe. During the last twenty-four hours the camp has been engulfed by successive tidal waves of Jews. I must tell you: I was shocked by Father and Mother today, and Mischa too. Father is completely helpless, and his collar has grown a lot too big for him over the last twenty-four hours, and the gray stubble of his beard is pathetic. But he waved a small Bible about this morning while we waited for hours and hours in the rain, and found a marvelous quotation from Joshua. They are in a big barracks now, a jam-packed human warehouse: people sleeping three to a bed on narrow iron bunks, no mattresses for the men, nowhere at all to store anything, children terrified and screaming, the greatest possible wretchedness. I shall try to get through it as best I can, I even feel quite strong and brave, although sometimes I can see nothing but blackness and nothing makes any sense at all.

Now for something practical. We must try to get Father some bread, since he doesn't eat hot food. You can still send registered "letter-parcels" from the provinces weighing up to 2 kilos. Please see if you can get one of them through to us. You won't think it impertinent of me to ask you straight out like this; needs must. Rye bread would be very welcome too. Don't send coupons here, we can't do anything with them. Mail them to Jacobs, Retiefstraat 11, and tell him that from Amsterdam he can still send parcels weighing up to 5 kilos, preferably registered. It's safest to address them to me: Dr. E. Hillesum, Assistant, Jewish Council, Westerbork Camp, Post Hoog-Halen, O, Drenthe. Top left: Barracks 34. Write us a postcard if you do send us something, then I can look out for it—

I hope I'll find a bed tonight, every square millimeter is taken. More later. Please pray a little for us.

Love,
Etty

Well, children, here I am again. The letter I started is back under my orange checked sleeping bag, and now I'm sitting in another corner of the camp carrying on this chat with you on a bit of paper that's turned up. I have just been with my papa. This is a historic moment for him—he ate a plateful of cabbage and this morning he even drank some milk, although he always swore that he'd rather go to Poland than drink milk. An angel of a stalwart Russian in the bed next to him guides him through every clumsy movement and whistles at night when he snores too loudly. Four hundred people from the hospital will apparently have to go on the next transport. Walking through the barracks, particularly the one with most of the old women, is an act of despair. One after another they clutch at you and implore, "I don't really have to go on this transport, do I?" and "Surely they won't take us away from here," and then always the same thing over and over—"Isn't there anything you can do for me?" Yesterday a very old woman, sick, nothing but skin and bones, asked me, "Do you think there will be medical assistance in Poland?" In the face of something like that, I feel like running away. It is almost beyond comprehension, the strength with which people whose lives are almost entirely behind them hang on to the wretched bits of carcass that are left. But they all want to live to see peace and see their children and families again, which is perfectly understandable, really—

Just when I was about to descend from my third-story heaven to solid ground this morning, Anne-Marie climbed up to me; she looked like an aviator in her beret and goggles.[31] She's on indoor duty in the barracks where I was assigned last year. She's doing extremely well; tell Swiep in particular.[32] She sleeps well, eats well, doesn't have any hard work, and is here on her own. That's very important; I can see in myself the effects of worry about the family. It gnaws at you worse than anything else. I haven't seen Mischa and Mother today; I've been in bed, and Mother's been laid up with a bit of an upset stomach. I always have a strong inner resistance to overcome, a kind of fear, before I can go inside their barracks, where the sour, fetid human reek hits you in the face. Sam de Wolff is in the same barracks as Mischa; I run across him now and then pottering about between the iron bunks.[33]

We are expecting a transport from the Hollandse Schouwburg any day now.[34] Everyone thinks it will be sent straight through to Poland. All we know about Jaap is that he is in the Schouwburg, nothing more.[35] I shall do whatever I possibly can to hold onto him here, but there's no way of forcing things to happen. Everyone has to accept the fate allotted to him; there's nothing else for it. Just now a woman who cleans for Kormann said to me, "You always look so radiant." But I feel just as I always have, wherever I've been. Of course I'm a little weary and worn down, and giddy with worry now and then. But everyone has worries here, so why shouldn't we share them and bear them together honestly? I am experiencing much that is good here. Each day Mechanicus, with whom I go for walks along the narrow, barren strip of earth between the ditch and the barbed wire, reads me what he has just written.[36] You develop friendships here that are enough for several lives at once. I still find time every day for a short philosophical conversation with Weinreb, a man who is a private world to himself with an atmosphere all his own that he manages to preserve no matter what happens.[37]

It's a shame I have so little time to write, there is so much

I want to tell you. I'll save it up for later, I promise. But now we must concern ourselves with cabbage, a favorite dish in these parts.

A little later

The cooking is good here; I won't hear a word against it. Children, I would so much like to know how you all are. Why don't I hear anything from Maria? Is it true, Maria, that Ernst is coming to visit us here? So Renate told me.[38] I meet Paul's mother now and then on some muddy little path or other, and we gossip for a few minutes. There is no time for real "visits," nor is there a quiet place anywhere to sit down together. People talk to each other in passing, outdoors. Really, one keeps walking about all day long—

Oh yes, there is something else, something the whole Jewish Council here is so full of that I put it completely out of my mind. The latest news (although it's sure to change again a few times): sixty of us may stay here, the other sixty must go back to Amsterdam, where they will get special "exemptions." Because my parents are here, naturally I am one of those who want to stay on, come what may. Most of us do, actually, since almost everyone has family here whom he can still protect a little by his presence. So you have a paradoxical situation: while each of us would give anything to get away from W., many of us would have to be thrown out before we'd go. People are terribly wound up. Debates, computations, laws of probability, are the order of the day. I keep well out of it. All this talking takes up energy and nothing comes of it in the end. Improbable though it may sound to you, I am really and truly the most taciturn person in the whole JC. People here fritter their energy away on the thousand irksome details that grind us down every day; they lose themselves in detail and drown. That's why they get driven off course and find existence pointless. The few big things that matter in life are what we have to keep in mind; the rest can be quietly abandoned. And you can find those few big things anywhere, you have to keep rediscovering them in yourself so that you can be renewed. And in spite of everything you always end up with the same conviction: life is good after all, it's not God's fault that things go awry sometimes, the cause lies in ourselves. And that's what stays with me, even now, even when I'm about to be packed off to Poland with my whole family.

And now I'm going to look for Mother and Mischa. 'Bye for now.

Last stage

I am sitting on my suitcase in our little kitchen, it's so full in here that not another mortal can enter. Now for a few practical details . . . Intermezzo: A nice man just came in who used to be one of Spier's subjects; he sat on another suitcase and suddenly we were right in the middle of chirology.[39] I meet quite a few of Spier's clients and pupils here. And we always say the same thing: what a mercy it is that he is no longer with us. Now for some business. I am enclosing a few more bread coupons. Would Frans take it badly if you telephoned and asked him to send us some more Sanovite biscuits? Is Frans still there, anyway? Mother eats hardly anything anymore, she cannot stand the bread here, and I should like to be able to give her a little Sanovite now and then. Is it a great bore for you, my making such a nuisance of myself? I hope the soap coupons haven't been used up yet; I always forget to send them. I do the washing here myself in a bucket outside the house, and we hang it up on a piece of string. A little primitive, but it does the job.

This letter is also for Mien Kuiper; I won't have a chance

to write her today.[40] Would you be kind enough to tell her that up to now, Sunday, none of her parcels have arrived? Her letters have come, so she knows the address. It would be a pity if anything of hers went astray; she also wrote that she has sent things twice. Please ask if she'd be kind enough to send tomatoes and other fresh things. Since there is a continuous sandstorm here, people are full of dust and completely dried up, so that they need fresh things even more than bread. I don't myself have any such craving. That's to be expected; ever since that police-raid transport I haven't been hungry, have had no sleep or anything. But I feel very well, all the same. One concentrates so much on others that one forgets oneself, and that's just as well. Ask Mien to give our best regards to Milli Ortmann; as soon as I can I'll write her too. Let's hope that Mischa gets out of Westerbork; being here won't do him any good in the long run, but I can't do anything with him while our parents are still at risk here. I shall now break off before I ruin my eyes permanently. Love to everyone dear to me—you know who they are well enough.

'Bye,
Etty

Would you be kind enough to send some postage stamps next time?

Christine,

We are sitting just now, Father and I, on a kind of stone drain. A glorious fresh breeze is blowing. In front of us, people with yellow stars are digging a moat to stop us from running away, and beyond that stretches the barbed wire. To the left, in the corner of the camp, the military police-man stands high up in his little hut on posts. We are black with sand; the breeze is a real sirocco. I have just lifted Father down from his second-tier bunk, and we are airing it a bit. I am very grateful that he has a bed to himself now; in the big barracks he would have gone to pieces within a week. We shall try somehow to pull each other through. Mother is admirable. It's almost unbelievable—she goes about just as spryly and neatly turned out as always. Today, for instance, she did a big wash in a bucket and hung the clothes out on a piece of string. Mischa's attachment to them both is touching. He lives in constant fear that they will have to go to Poland, and says there's no question but that he'll go with them. However, everything will work out. Until further notice I'm keeping them here for certain. Our greatest worries are for Mischa; we are afraid that things will soon get too much for him. It is really beyond comprehension why people don't all go mad here.

Anyway. Now to come to the point. This morning a very welcome parcel arrived from Simon.[41] Nothing from you; we'll just have to wait a little longer. Perhaps it's as well that everything is being sent via the Jewish Council. Mother is looking forward to your shrimp pies. How do you like that? We're going in for special orders now. This morning she said how wonderful it would be if we could have something spicy to eat for once, and immediately Mevrouw de Groot from Ceintuurbaan said that she still

65

had lots of spicy things left. Oh well, I am noting it all down like a dutiful secretary. And do you know, we can again change bread and butter coupons in the canteen here. If you have any left over, you might be kind enough to send a few. Half the camp has lectured Father about eating something hot, but so far he hasn't managed to.

Now we are right in the middle of a sandstorm; can you read my writing? Everything here is mad and incredible and desperate and comical, all at the same time. Everything I write is all mixed up too, but that's the way things are. Oh yes: it's quite possible that I will shortly be stripped of my privileged position, because the Jewish Council here is about to be dissolved. Then I won't be able to write as often as I would like. But we'll still have a writing day once every two weeks, so you'll go on hearing from us. And now we must leave our nice stone seat; otherwise we'll develop galloping consumption. Let us hope that a time will come when we'll be able to tell you everything in person, let us truly hope for that. And yes, please pray for us a little. And thank you for everything.

Much love,
Etty

Very dearest Milli,

First for something absolutely crucial: the *Zentralstelle* must tell our camp commandant through official channels that my parents and Mischa are to be kept on here. Otherwise it won't be any use at all.

We have managed to survive the latest transport night: Mischa has been "deferred" temporarily, and we've hung on to my parents, too, because they are on the "parents' list" of Westerbork staff. But the list is not something you can rely on. Next week the battle starts all over again. If they go on sending out one transport a week, it will be impossible to hold my parents back without some intervention from outside. Last night the Hollandse Schouwburg lot arrived, and I stood guard all night because we were expecting Jaap. To our utter delight he didn't turn up. We heard a vague report that he had been kept back because he was on the Meijer list (what sort of list is that, for heaven's sake?). At five o'clock in the morning I forced my way into the hospital to make sure they weren't going to drag Father off by accident and to tell him the joyful news about Jaap. Lots of the sick who were due to leave were being dressed by the male nurses. The long train of dilapidated boxcars had stood waiting the whole day. Empty cattle cars, each with a bucket in the middle. Paper mattresses on the floor for the sick. After I'd been to see Father I walked right across the camp to Mother's large barracks, where almost everyone was getting ready to leave. The people were dignified, calm, and disciplined. I saw off a great many good friends. Just now I went back again to Mother's. She was lying on her narrow iron soldier's bed in a state of exhaustion. After a transport night like that, we all feel sick and and ready to drop. Then we take a deep breath and go on with life until the next transport. I keep hoping and hoping that there will be some message from the *Zentralstelle*. My parents are really bearing up splendidly. Inwardly they are preparing for Poland. They make few demands and do not complain; I am terribly proud of them. Mischa is the same as ever. He is a bit grubby and now and then gets very worked up, and he never turns up on time for the roll calls. But his wonderful sense of humor hasn't deserted him even here.

I got your letter and the one from Grete and Cor as well. You are all being terribly kind. Many thanks for the parcels. What a nuisance we must be to you, it often weighs on my mind. Anyway, 'bye for now.

Love,
Etty

Little Father Han, Käthe, Maria, Hans,

Just a telegram-style message for you out of the blue. Stood guard last night to watch out for Jaap. He wasn't in the Schouwburg transport; we were delirious with joy. In the morning another big transport left. I even went to the hospital at five o'clock to make sure they hadn't taken Father along by mistake—there are plenty of mistakes. Then to Mother's big barracks, where she was lying on her cramped soldier's bed. She was delighted by the news about Jaap. My parents are taking things nobly, I am very proud of them. They don't even dread Poland anymore— they say. I hope I can keep them here, but nothing is certain. In a few days you can drift far from your former moorings. New and powerful forces enter into you. Accepting your own doom needs inner strength.

I got a letter from Leguit which touched me very much. He is another one of those people who make you want to survive just so you can see them again later on. He enclosed a quotation from Dr. Korff: "And yet God is love." I completely agree, and it is truer now than ever. Leguit also wrote: "It would surprise me if you had enough resilience of spirit left to spare even half an ear for those who have stayed behind." I have all my ears and all my attention to spare for you. I go on living with you just as before, and pause with you now and then to rest from all that overwhelms me here. It is more difficult for you to digest the events at Westerbork than for us. I have noticed that in every situation, even the most difficult, man generates new faculties that help him go on living. As far as that is concerned, God is merciful enough. And for the rest: several suicides last night before the transport, with razors and so on. This morning, while I stood at the tub with a colleague,

I said with great emotion something like this: "The realms of the soul and the spirit are so spacious and unending that this little bit of physical discomfort and suffering really doesn't matter all that much. I do not feel I have been robbed of my freedom; essentially no one can do me any harm at all." Yes, children, that's how it is, I am in a strange state of mournful contentment. If I once wrote you a desperate letter, don't take it too much to heart; it expressed only a brief moment. It's true you can suffer, but that need not make you desperate. And now I'm going to jump in at the deep end again; I'm off to the hospital with a little tin box for my beloved father under one arm and my official folder under the other. I shall find many empty beds there after this transport. Be of good cheer, my dear good friends. How is Cousin Wegerif? And Käthe, are you being good? And isn't Father Han being silent to a fault? Hannes's mother did *not* go to Theresienstadt. Regards to Adri from Ilse B.

'Bye!

Christine, my dear,

I am stealing a few moments in the sun to scribble to various friends. It is a glorious day—how different life suddenly looks! I am so glad my work is in the hospital area; it means I can drop in on Father whenever I like. And when I can't go inside his barracks, we can have a little chat through his open window, since his bed is right next to it. I have just taken him your letters; he was very pleased. Now I have your note in front of me. I gave an Indian whoop of joy over the goggles; without them our eyes are completely ruined here. How nice of you to send them on your own initiative! It's so sweet, the way you look after us. I'm sure you people in the outside world have enough troubles of your own without adding all of ours. Your letter to Mischa was lovely. Father has it now and will hand it on when Mischa visits him today.

(Half an hour later. Just now a picturesque interlude: A good friend of mine from Amsterdam, a talented young musician, came past in filthy overalls with a barrowful of sand. Between the barbed wire and the little pieces of string on which the dingy washing has been hung out to dry, we delivered ourselves of philosophical observations concerning the marvels and mysteries of this earthly existence. Let's hope that not too many more friends come past with barrows, since I have a lot more to write you.)

An end will come soon enough to all the scribbling. I am only too grateful that I'm allowed to stay on. Have I already told you that of the hundred and twenty people working for the Jewish Council, sixty *must* go home? Luckily I am not one of the sixty, so I can keep on protecting my parents as best I can. You see, there is always new cause for satisfaction. In Amsterdam the fight for Barneveld continues. I hope and pray that it will work out. I myself would ten times rather go to Poland or wherever, if only I am able to get my dear ones away from this place first. Well, we must simply have patience—which, indeed, we already do have in plenty.

When I am not allowed to write anymore, I'll still be able to send a postcard following the arrival of a parcel, with the words "Parcel received"—nothing else. So if a meaningless card like that comes, you'll know why. And something else: we are permitted to send telegrams to the Jewish Council to ask for things we need—also without further comment.

But we are forbidden to be specific; we can only put something like "food" in the telegram. So let's agree now on, for example: book = butter, writing = jam, ink = rye bread, shoelaces = fruit. (If it comes to the point where I have to send telegrams like that, then you will get in touch with Simon, won't you?)

Do you know, we can utter a lot of "important words" here without turning a hair. I can name fruit, tomatoes, and things like that with no difficulty at all. Yet I don't even know if you in the outside world have any of these. You must not think it presumptuous if we ask for impossible things; please remember it is due to ignorance. What Father, for instance, badly needs is fruit and green vegetables. We get so dried up here because of the continuous sandstorms. The water is not very good either; we are advised not to drink too much of it because of the "camp sicknesses," and everything else available to drink is awful. I am pretty sure that Mother has lots of different bottled drinks in the Deventer house, but it would probably be quite a business to get them over here. I have the feeling that we are giving you a lot of trouble, but it's all to keep each other alive. Oh Christine, just imagine, a time may come once more when we can tell each other everything. And if we survive, we will surely be grateful that we were present at one of the many fronts in Europe, where we could share some part of all the suffering. Yesterday the man who regularly cuts Father's hair said to me, "You're the sort of person who makes something of her life in any circumstances."

Father is marvelous, and wonderfully resigned. Yesterday morning all the beds were standing outside his barracks, in the sand blowing about between two great empty hospital buildings. It looked like an open-air sanatorium. Walking past, I heard Father's hearty laughter ringing out over the entire area. He has nice people around him who search over and over for all the little things that, with some *grandezza* and a certain nonchalance, he loses daily. There is a journalist, Philip Mechanicus, a stylish, strong-minded character, who regularly drops by and chats with him. Father has also come across many old student friends here. He studies the Bible with great concentration, comparing the French, Greek, and Dutch versions. I brought him the writings of Meister Eckhart and another couple of books I had here. He doesn't eat all that much; we are able to share out quite a lot of his bread. It's a good thing, since we are all beginning to feel the pinch badly now that the outside world, which used to send supplies regularly, has shrunk so much. For all the families and acquaintances of most Jews are here now.

I'm going to abandon my sunny, windy little corner and the well I'm sitting on. I shall walk past Father's window and then go to take pot luck in my barracks. We are very, very happy Jaap isn't here yet; it's nice that you went to look him up. When the transport from the Hollandse Schouwburg arrived a few nights ago, I stood watch all

73

night to catch him. Thank God it wasn't necessary. I'll write more later; I won't send this letter off until your parcel arrives. Good-bye for now.

5:30 p.m.

If you only knew what it means here just to be able to be in a little room all by yourself. I am sitting in such a room now and will finally be able to finish answering your letter. Are you still interested in special requests? It would make me radiantly happy if you could send paper handkerchiefs. People here have chronic colds, aggravated by the climate, and regular handkerchiefs get filthier rather than cleaner when you wash them. The hygiene problem is really the most desperate of all. Father complains bitterly that he is the biggest gypsy in Westerbork; he doesn't see that everyone else is in the same boat. Can you still get sanitary napkins? And ordinary rolls of bandages? An obstinate eczema that I once had for a few years on my right hand has flared up again, and I keep it bandaged because of the dust. I ask you for all these things with a heavy heart; for I know they're not easy to come by, are they? And oh yes, if there's still one of our little pots of jam there, perhaps it also could make the trip here in the course of time. One should avoid having too many special requests these days, I think. But that's the difficult part, you see. I wouldn't beg favors for myself, but I would turn the world upside down to get my parents something to lighten their lives a little. There you are. We wish you all a very nice holiday. Father's writing day is tomorrow; I think he plans a letter to you. It will take a week to arrive; it's got to pass a special censor. Forgive my saying everything in such a muddle, that's what these surroundings do to one. I hope I can still write you often, but it looks as if that won't be possible much longer. I don't need writing paper yet.

Lots of love, and thanks for everything,
Etty

. . .

P.S. from Mother: Perhaps you would be kind enough some time to get in touch with Gantvoort, the baker, private address c/o Larese, 23 Sweelinckstraat. He once said that he would like to bake something. Sorry and all that, but it isn't for myself.

Jopie, Klaas, my dear friends,[42]

Here I am on the third tier of this bunk hurrying to unleash a veritable riot of writing, for in a few days' time it'll be the end of the line for my scribblings. I'll have become a "camp inmate," allowed to write just one letter a fortnight, and unsealed at that. And there are still a couple of little things I must talk to you about. Did I really send a letter that made it look as if all my courage had gone? I can hardly believe it. There are moments, it's true, when I feel things can't go on. But they do go on, you gradually learn that as well. Though the landscape around you may appear different: there is a lowering black sky overhead and a great shift in your outlook on life and your heart feels gray and a thousand years old. But it is not always like that. A human being is a remarkable thing. The misery here is really indescribable. People live in those big barracks like so many rats in a sewer. There are many dying children. But there are many healthy ones, too.

One night last week a transport of prisoners passed through here. Thin, waxen faces. I have never seen so much exhaustion and fatigue as I did that night. They were being "processed": registration, more registration, frisking by half-grown NSB men, quarantine, a foretaste of martyrdom lasting hours and hours.[43] Early in the morning they were crammed into empty freight cars. Then another long wait while the train was boarded up. And then three days' travel eastwards. Paper "mattresses" on the floor for the sick. For the rest, bare boards with a bucket in the middle and roughly seventy people to a sealed car. A rucksack each was all they were allowed to take. How many, I wondered, would reach their destination alive? And my parents are preparing themselves for just such a journey unless something comes of Barneveld after all.

Last time I saw my father, we went for a walk in the dusty, sandy wasteland. He is so sweet, and wonderfully resigned. Very pleasantly, calmly, and quite casually, he said, "You know, I would like to get to Poland as quickly as possible. Then it will all be over and done with and I won't have to continue with this undignified existence. After all, why should I be spared from what has happened to thousands of others?" Later we joked about our surroundings. Westerbork really is nothing but desert, despite a few lupins and campions and decorative birds which look like seagulls. "Jews in a desert, we know that sort of landscape from before." It really gets you down, having such a nice little father, you sometimes feel there is no hope at all.

But these are passing moods. There are other sorts, too, when a few of us laugh together and marvel at all sorts of things. And then we keep meeting lots of relatives whom we haven't seen for years—lawyers, a librarian, and so on—pushing wheelbarrows full of sand, in untidy, ill-fitting overalls, and we just look at each other and don't say much. A young, sad Dutch police officer told me one transport night, "I lose two kilos during a night like this, and all *I* have to do is to listen, look, and keep my mouth shut." And that's why I don't like to write about it, either. But I am digressing. All I wanted to say is this: The misery here is quite terrible; and yet, late at night when the day has slunk away into the depths behind me, I often walk with a spring in my step along the barbed wire. And then time and again, it soars straight from my heart—I can't help it, that's just the way it is, like some elementary force—the feeling that life is glorious and magnificent, and that one day we shall be building a whole new world. Against every new outrage and every fresh horror, we shall put up one more piece of love and goodness, drawing strength from within ourselves. We may suffer, but we must not succumb. And if we should survive unhurt in body and soul, but above all in soul, without bitterness and without hatred, then we shall have a right to a say after the war. Maybe I am an ambitious woman: I would like to have just a tiny little bit of a say.

You speak about suicide, and about mothers and children. Yes, I know what you mean, but I find it a morbid subject. There is a limit to suffering; perhaps no human being is given more to bear than he can shoulder; beyond a certain point we just die. People are dying here even now of a broken spirit, because they can no longer find any meaning in life, young people. The old ones are rooted in firmer soil and accept their fate with dignity and calm. You see so many different sorts of people here, and so many different attitudes to the hardest, the ultimate questions . . .

I shall try to convey to you how I feel, but am not sure if my metaphor is right. When a spider spins its web, does it not cast the main threads ahead of itself, and then follow along them from behind? The main path of my life stretches like a long journey before me and already reaches into another world. It is just as if everything that happens here and that is still to happen were somehow discounted inside me. As if I had been through it already, and was now helping to build a new and different society. Life here hardly touches my deepest resources—physically, perhaps, you do decline a little, and sometimes you are infinitely sad—but fundamentally you keep growing stronger. I just hope that it can be the same for you and all my friends. We need it, for we still have so much to experience together and so much work to do. And so I call upon you: stay at your inner post, and please do not feel sorry or sad for me, there is no reason to. The Levies are having a hard time, but they have enough inner reserves to pull them through despite their poor physical state. Many of the children here are very dirty. That is one of our biggest problems—hygiene. I'll write again and tell you more about them. I enclose a scribbled note I began to write to Father and Mother, but didn't have to send; you might find some of it interesting.

I have one request, if you don't think it too immodest: a pillow or some old cushion; the straw gets a little hard in the end. But you are not allowed to send parcels weighing more than two kilos from the provinces, and a pillow probably weighs more than that. So if you happen to be in Amsterdam and should call at Pa Han's (please don't abandon him, and do show him this letter), you might perhaps send it from some post office there. Otherwise, my only wish is that you are all well and in good spirits, and send me a few kind words from time to time.

Lots and lots of love,
Etty

Westerbork, [Monday], 5 July [1943]

I must try to conjure up a letter in haste, for if tomorrow or the day after I am not allowed to write anymore, I shall regret not doing it now. It's a difficult day. A transport leaves tomorrow morning, and last night I heard that my parents were on the list. Herman B. whispered it in my ear as I sat on the edge of Father's bed having a cosy chat— Father all unsuspecting. I didn't say anything and immediately went to see the various authorities. I was told that my parents are still safe, but you can't be certain until the last minute. I shall keep as close a watch as I can until tomorrow morning. Tonight another transport is coming in from Amsterdam, so I'll be up then in any case. Mechanicus, with whom I have struck up a firm friendship in a short time, is also on the list; we are still trying everything we can. Weinreb was taken away some time ago— by car to the Hague in the care of a couple of VIPs. You mustn't become too attached to people here.

This morning I worked in the punishment barracks, where people are in special custody, and took news back from the detainees to their relatives in the camp. I have just been to see Father again. He was lying down, reasonably content, reading a French novel and unaware that his name still has to be taken off the list. The hardest labor camp is better than this suspense every week. It didn't bother me so much before, because I had accepted the fact that I would be going to Poland. But living in fear for your loved ones, knowing that an infinitely long martyrdom is in store for them while your own life here stays relatively idyllic, is something few can bear. I sometimes feel like quietly packing my rucksack and getting onto the next transport to the East. But enough; it's not right for a human being to take the easy way out.

Tuesday morning

It is ten o'clock. I am sitting in our empty workroom; it is wonderfully peaceful; most of my colleagues are asleep in their barracks. A couple of boys are leaning on the windowsill gazing gloomily at the locomotive, which is belching clouds of smoke again. The rest of the train is hidden from view behind a low barracks. People have been busy loading the freight cars since six o'clock this morning; the train is ready to pull out. I feel as if I've just gone through labor on my parents' behalf; this time we managed once again to keep them off the train. Otherwise I find it difficult to say honestly how I feel.

Yesterday was a day like no other. Never before have I taken a hand in "fixing" it to keep someone off the transport. I lack all talent for diplomacy, but yesterday I did my bit for Mechanicus. What exactly it was that I did, I'm not sure. I went to all sorts of officials. Suddenly I found myself walking around with a mysterious gentleman I've never seen before who looked like a white slave trafficker in a French film. With this gentleman I went to all sorts of camp VIPs who are usually not available, especially before a transport. But this time invisible doors opened: one moment I had an interview with the *Registrator* and the next I was appearing before a senile little man who presumably holds a mysterious position of power and can get people off the transport even when all seems lost. There is a sort of "underworld" here in Westerbork; yesterday I sensed something of it, I don't know how it all fits together, I don't think it's a savory story—Anyway, I trudged around the whole day, while my parents were entrusted to Kormann's

81

watchful eye and to the staff of the Jewish Council, who assured me that everything would be all right this time.

As far as Mechanicus was concerned, things were in doubt until the very last moment. I helped him pack his bags, sewed a few buttons on his suit. He said, "I've grown softer here in this camp, everyone has become the same for me, they are all like blades of grass, bending to the storm, lying flat under the hurricane." He also said, "If I survive this time, I shall emerge a more mature and deeper person, and if I die, then I shall die a more mature and deeper one." Later my father said as I patted the top of his head, now almost white, "If I get my call-up tonight, truly I won't be upset, I'll leave quite peacefully." (People usually get their call-up in the night, a few hours before the transport leaves.)

At eight o'clock I walked about with Mother, said goodbye to various friends who had to go, then went for a walk with Liesl and Werner. At about ten o'clock I sat down with Jopie, who looks gray with fatigue. And after that I really couldn't stand up any longer. I excused myself from night work and let things take their course. This morning at eight o'clock Jopie came by and told me through the window that my parents were still here, that Jaap didn't arrive last night (we were expecting people from the NIZ), and that Mechanicus is *not* on transport.[44] And now it is eleven o'clock and I am going to the hospital, where I shall find a lot of empty beds. A day like yesterday is a killer, and next week the same thing starts all over again.

Late afternoon

Well, children, here I am again on the top bunk, three tiers up. This afternoon, for a change, I fainted in the middle of a large, stuffy barracks. It serves as a reminder that there are limits to one's physical strength. In addition to the hospital barracks, I have now been assigned the punishment barracks as well. Since half our colleagues have gone back to Amsterdam, there are many jobs to cover. Then Kormann told me that my parents must still expect to be put on transport next week. It will become more and more difficult to keep people back—but you never know in advance, and that is precisely what saps you, the uncertainty until the last minute. Then I went to see Mother, who was feeling dizzy and sick herself; and then I felt I had reached the end of my tether and fainted. Tomorrow, things will be better. I suddenly remember that it's the "summer holidays" in the outside world. Do you have any plans? You will tell me everything, won't you? Maria, thank you for your letter! It was exactly what a letter from you ought to be. If I am allowed to write tomorrow, I'll send you another scrawl; otherwise I shall keep quiet for the time being—

We learn everything from the doctors here. What a desperate state of affairs. We have a surfeit of doctors, who are unable to do anything useful. Jan Zeeman's father is here too!

Good-bye! Be strong!
Etty

Milli darling,

Just a brief cry of distress. I did start a letter to you and Mien, but a letter gets out of date here even as you write it. Today my strength failed me for the first time and I fainted right in the middle of a big barracks. This morning yet another transport of 2,500 left. I managed with difficulty to keep my parents off it, but things are getting quite desperate. Good friends of mine here, who have what is called influence, told me in confidence this morning that my parents must make ready for next week's transport. Slowly but steadily the camp is being sucked dry. Without some miracle from outside, it will all be over in a week or two. What we really want is to get Mischa, who is determined to stick with his parents and face certain doom, away from here. Is it really true that he could have gone to Barneveld by himself? And wouldn't it still be possible, even if our parents don't go to B., for him to get an order telling him that he *must* go? Even though, to be honest, I know quite well that nothing will make him go without his parents. "If they are sent on transport, that'll be the end of me too," he keeps saying. Between ourselves, it's all a long tale of woe. And the worst part is that you are able to do so much less for your people than they expect. Six months ago it would probably still have been fairly simple to keep them back here and make them feel quite at home, but I am becoming more helpless all the time. You yourselves know very well what sort of feeling that is. I won't write more now, for I can see this is not going to be a sunny letter.

You are such dears; all the trouble and effort and worry we are causing you weigh heavily on my conscience. I have just read Cor's letter to Mischa. A Kuiper-Glassner parcel has arrived, but no Kuiper-Ortmann parcel. It's sad when parcels you have prepared with so much care and love don't get through, but I think that everything else has arrived. It's all so welcome, and I often wonder how you manage to bring it off, since things can't be that easy with you either. We have also received a large box of tomatoes and cucumbers without the sender's name. So I don't know who it was, but report arrival in any case.

I must cut this short, dearest friend. I am feeling a bit downhearted, but things are bound to be better tomorrow. Regards to Grete and Cor.

Love,
Etty

Sooner or later I won't be allowed to write more than once every two weeks, so if you suddenly stop getting any signs of life from me, you'll know there was nothing I could do about it.

Thursday afternoon, [*8 July 1943*]

Hello! I've been telling myself for the past half hour, half asleep, to write some more to you. Every writing day is an event: there's been nothing definite said yet about having to stop writing. And so I scribble on.

A few things before I forget them. Leo Krijn has been sent through; leaving won't matter very much to him. His brother, who is still here, said to me yesterday, "He has the naïve hope that he will find his wife and son again over there."

Herman B. is worried; for a whole week he has heard nothing from Wiep and his mother. Is anything the matter? He is as well as always. He doggedly feeds my father cucumbers and tomatoes all day long. I pity Father sometimes because he's not allowed out of the barracks, but it doesn't seem to bother him very much, the clouds of dust outside hold no attraction for him.

I took Swiep's parcel to Anne-Marie. She was so nice that I've arranged to meet her one evening; she wants to introduce me to a sociable Russian professor so we can have a bit of a chat.

My right hand is bandaged up because of the eczema, and that's why I am writing even less legibly than usual. Now you'll have to retouch even more letters, dear Father Han. Thank you for your lovely letter. I would find it hard to bear if Käthe really went away. Is it irrevocable? Please don't let it be!

At the moment I am lying in the middle of a battlefield of sick women. The wrong kind of bacillus is raging through our barracks, we have all got the "runs," as it is poetically termed. I am quite pleased to be immobilized; it gives me a chance to write to you. I gather from Grete

Wendelsgelst's latest report,[45] which I got this morning, that my family will be able to stay here after all. Yesterday it appeared that they had to go.

After I had fainted twice on the same day, I made up my mind to start a new life without all these tensions. I was also beginning to suffer from "stampitis": they stamp your papers with red, green, and blue identification marks; you can talk about them for twenty-four hours at a stretch—it is an inexhaustible subject. Jopie is really sick of stampitis—when he hears the word *stamp*, he wants to vomit. At the moment feelings are at fever pitch: all stamps, all colors, have been suspended; there is to be a regrouping. What the next transport will look like no one knows—the lists still have to be made up, and in the process all kinds of things are bound to go on behind the scenes. They are playing a game with us, but we allow them to do so, and that will be our shame for generations to come. I told you a few days ago something about a senile little man for whom closed doors mysteriously opened. He's really a pleasant little man; he served as a courier in the Great War and among other things was a friend of Archbishop Söderblom.[46] He is the only person allowed to call unannounced on the commandant—who even returns his visits, which is a very great honor here, God help us. Yesterday I walked with him and Mechanicus for a couple of hours, and he came up with reminiscences about Poincaré and the Queen; no lesser person would do for him. But he also said something very much to the point: "In Westerbork there is only one service that's equitable: the water supply. It provides water for 10,000 Jews, and each one gets the same amount."

You don't mind my writing everything a bit mixed up, do you? It's because I am so sleepy. You see, I keep striking the same chords even here. Experience has shown me forcibly: if you allow yourself to get involved in all the tensions here each week, then in three weeks you're done for, absolutely done for. And when it's finally your turn to go off in the Moscow direction, you're just not able to make it anymore. So I am trying to live my life away from all the green, red, and blue stamps and transport lists.

Now and then I join the gulls. In their movements through the great cloudy skies one suspects laws, eternal laws of another order than the laws we humans make. This afternoon Jopie, who feels thoroughly sick and all in, stood together with his sister-in-arms Etty for at least a quarter of an hour looking up at one of these black and silver birds as it moved among the massive deep-blue rain clouds. We suddenly felt a lot less oppressed.

One should be able to write fairy stories here. It sounds strange, but if you wanted to convey something of Westerbork life you could do it best in that form. The misery here is so beyond all bounds of reality that it has become unreal. Sometimes I walk through the camp laughing secretly to myself because of the completely grotesque circumstances. One would have to be a very great poet indeed to describe them; perhaps in about ten years I might get somewhere near it.

In the evening

I have to stop right in the middle of the fairy tales—

Next morning

People live an episodic life here; I have a quarter of an hour to spare, so another few words. Yes, really, it's true, there are compassionate laws in nature, if only we can keep a feeling for their rhythm. I notice that afresh each time in myself: when I am at the limits of despair, unable, I am sure, to go on, suddenly the balance shifts over to the other side and I can laugh and take life as it comes. After feeling really low for ages, you can suddenly rise so high above earthly misery that you feel lighter and more liberated than ever before in your life. I am now very well again, but for a few days I was quite desperate. Equilibrium is restored time and again. Ah, children, we live in a strange world—

It is a complete madhouse here; we shall have to feel ashamed of it for three hundred years. The *Dienstleiters* themselves now have to draw up the transport lists.[47] Meetings, panics—it's all horrible. In the middle of this game with human lives, an order suddenly from the commandant: the *Dienstleiters* must present themselves that evening at the first night of a cabaret which is being put on here. They stared open-mouthed, but they had to go home and dress in their best clothes. And then in the evening they sit in the registration hall, where Max Ehrlich, Chaya Goldstein, Willy Rosen, and others give a performance.[48] In the first row, the commandant with his guests. Behind him, Professor Cohen.[49] The rest of the hall full. People laughing until they cried—oh yes, cried. On days when the people from Amsterdam pour into the camp, we put up a kind of wooden barrier in the big reception hall to hold them back if the crush becomes too great. During the cabaret this same barrier served as a piece of decor on the stage; Max Ehrlich leaned over it to sing his little songs. I wasn't there myself, but Kormann just told me about it, adding, "This whole business is slowly driving me to the edge of despair."

I will have to put an end to this letter, otherwise I won't be able to send it off. I must just think what else I should add. I received a cigar box full of tomatoes from Gera;[50] please thank her if you see her; I can't write as many letters as before. Mevrouw Nethe's Jim is also here from Mien's house, so I know the latest news.[51] Oh yes, Father Han, please send me ten guilders in a letter; even now money can sometimes come in very useful, however silly that may sound. They are still working on getting a short leave for us in order "finally" to settle our affairs. If it comes off, it will be a lovely extra gift, but I don't count on it any longer. If I am allowed to write tomorrow, I'll send another scribble; otherwise you must have a little patience—

However improbable it may sound: I am more saddened by what happens in the outside world than by events on the battlefield here. I remember a lunch with Johannes Brouwer; he was a sensitive man—who was here and then suddenly sent away.[52]

'Bye!
Etty

Dearest Christine,

I am on night duty now, so if no great panic occurs at my little table, I can scribble one or two words between business. In any case I want to send off a letter this evening so that your sister gets it in time. Do forgive me if this is all somewhat incoherent.

Christine, that Groningen cake! It was princely. Altogether it was such a magnificent parcel. I immediately gave Father a few small slices and half a bar of chocolate. It's marvelous, I just run over to him, five minutes from my barracks, pass him something through the window, and run back again. By holding on to one's people here, you can look after them and keep them going—with the help of the outside world. Mischa was there when I unpacked the parcel; he beamed. You had prepared it with such care and love, it sustains us—not just the contents, but also the thought that there are people who so much want to help us. Meanwhile another parcel has arrived from the Jewish Council in Deventer with glorious rye bread from Gantvoort. I always give half to Mother, who shares it with Mischa, and keep the other half for Father.

Tense and stirring days behind us. Father was on the transport list. We were able to get him off once again. I must explain that the call-ups for the transport come in the middle of the night, a few hours before the train leaves. If people are still needed at the last minute to fill the quotas, then Jews are seized here and there at random from the barracks. And that's why the days before the transport are so nerve-racking. The day afterwards I fainted twice, but I'm fine again now—until the next transport. Sunday evening while I was sitting talking on the edge of Father's bed, an acquaintance suddenly whispered in my ear: "Your father is on the list." People are afraid on such occasions to tell you the truth. And all Monday that long row of un-painted freight cars stood there, about seventy people—men, women, invalids, babies—squashed into each one, the doors slammed shut, a little air coming through the air holes and the broken planks, paper mattresses on the floor for the sick; for the rest only a hard floor, a bucket in the middle, and a three-day journey ahead. Can you imagine what that means? I have got used to the idea that I'll have to go myself one day. Above all else in the world I wish I could spare my parents and my brothers. But you can't play the ostrich here; a transport leaves every week and the quota must be filled. Just a little while longer and all our turns will come. My father takes it very quietly. "What all those thousands before us have borne, we can also bear," he says. I am grateful to have him here still, but on Mon-day the misery starts all over again. However—according to a report I received today from a good friend who is work-ing on our behalf—it seems that something is being done for us from the Hague after all.

Father and Mother give me a great deal of pleasure, for they are coping in their own ways; I admire them tremen-dously. Father now has two pupils in his hospital barracks, one boy who is not too ill and one who is very sick. Both want to learn a little Greek and Latin as a distraction, and he takes pleasure in giving them lessons for two hours a day, going through Homer, Ovid, and Sallust. For the rest, he reads a great deal, philosophizes with ancient rabbis and old student friends, and now and then strolls with his daughter through the dusty sand of the hospital grounds. Oh Christine, if only they could stay here in case nothing comes of Barneveld. There might be a chance of getting through here with the help of the outside world, however difficult everything may be. But once they're on the train, then I expect nothing but an endless martyrdom—We shall just have to wait and see—

A little later

Oh yes, the soap powder—I'd love it. Something like that is almost more important than food, the crowding has compelled such a poor state of hygiene. We wash our clothes often enough, in a variety of buckets obtained with difficulty. The clothes don't get much cleaner, it's true, but the idea that you have done a wash makes you feel a bit better—

I don't answer your letters as regularly as you answer mine because it's almost impossible here. Mischa's barracks is number 62.

The end of my duty; I shall rush over to my barracks. I have a fever and something poetically termed the runs; half the camp has got it at the moment, but I never like staying in bed, I prefer making myself useful.

What did I tell you? A messy, incoherent letter. Writing will really be coming to an end soon. I've heard that we're no longer allowed to acknowledge private parcels from the provinces with a postcard. If I write "Parcel received" to Simon, then I mean a parcel from the Jewish Council, but if I write "Little parcel," then I mean it's from you—although it would be more appropriate the other way around, as far as the size is concerned.

Much, much love from us all. We got a nice letter from van Kuyk.

Have a good holiday.

'Bye!
Etty

Milli, my priceless Milli,

I could fling my arms around your neck! Poor lamb, I keep sending you such terrible letters. Today the report from Grete, in which she says that the papers are on their way. We had heard nothing about it. Now there are high hopes that we'll be able to keep my parents here. All stamps have been declared invalid, everyone is due for transport except those whose affairs are still being considered in the Hague. And oh, Milli, I'd much sooner not see them in the freight cars, though I don't mind for myself. Well, we'll have to wait and see. In great haste. At the moment I'm not all that well: temperature, diarrhea—but half the camp has it. I'll send Wegerif a fuller letter tonight meant for you all. Hug Grete for her lovely letter. All of you are so kind even though you have worries enough yourselves. I am on the trail of your Aunt Hermine; I'll call on her tomorrow. It's all very well, but they ought to have left the old people in peace. How are all of you? Just think, Cor now lives so close to you! No, there's no chance that you might be able to come here. Thanks for everything. Won't you please ask Wegerif to reimburse you for all the expenses you have had? Although what you have done for us is really beyond price! In haste. More later, if it's still allowed.

'Bye,
Etty

Poor Milli,

I am so sorry for you, you have done so much running about and worked so hard. Barneveld is off, and off for Mischa, too. Father and Mother are on transport; Mischa has permission to stay but doesn't want to. It's getting very difficult to keep him quiet. He says: "I'm going to go and tell the commandant he is a murderer." We have to watch out that he doesn't do anything dangerous. Rauter's secretary is here in the camp at the moment and Mother was specially summoned to be given the news. She was told expressly that they are now due for transport on Tuesday. Whether anything can still be done from here, I don't know, I'll have to see. Our "parents' list" is unreliable right now; I don't even know whether my parents still come under that heading after the orders from the Hague. I just hope that some luggage will reach us from Amsterdam in time, although—we are more and more certain of this— everything is taken away from you anyway.

Let me arrange with you now something I've already written to Nethe. If Mother and Father leave next Tuesday and I am no longer allowed to write, then I shall wire Nethe. (We can still send certain specified telegrams to Jews in mixed marriages; they are delivered by courier.) My message will say, "Send two winter coats." If Mischa has gone as well, then I'll wire, "Send three winter coats." In the same way that Mischa wants to go out of love for his parents. I won't be going—out of a different kind of love. Perhaps it is a more cowardly love, but I myself feel strong. I believe that it is easier to pray for people from a distance than to see them suffer right next to you.

Should you get one of those telegrams, then please pass the news on to our friends in Amsterdam and also to Mejuffrouw J. C. J. C. van Nooten, Noorderbergersingel 7, Deventer, and to Mevrouw M. Gans, Roodenburgerstraat 60, Leiden. If it is at all possible I shall write again. If they are still here and I am not allowed to write, then I shall wire, "Send handkerchiefs." All right? Alas, one more sad bit of news: your Aunt Hermine is no longer here. I am so sorry, Milli my dear, that I have nothing but gloomy news.

Good-bye.
Love,
Etty

Maria, hello,

Ten thousand have passed through this place, the clothed and the naked, the old and the young, the sick and the healthy—and I am left to live and work and stay cheerful. It will be my parents' turn to leave soon, if by some miracle not this week, then certainly one of the next. And I must learn to accept this as well. Mischa insists on going along with them, and it seems to me that he probably should; if he has to watch our parents leave this place, it will totally unhinge him. I shan't go, I just can't. It is easier to pray for someone from a distance than to see him suffer by your side. It is not fear of Poland that keeps me from going along with my parents, but fear of seeing them suffer. And that, too, is cowardice.

This is something people refuse to admit to themselves: at a given point you can no longer *do*, but can only *be* and accept. And although that is something I learned a long time ago, I also know that one can only accept for oneself and not for others. And that's what is so desperately difficult for me here. Mother and Mischa still want to "do," to turn the whole world upside down, but I know we can't do anything about it. I have never been able to "do" anything; I can only let things take their course and if need be, suffer. This is where my strength lies, and it is great strength indeed. But for myself, not for others.

Mother and Father have definitely been turned down for Barneveld; we heard the news yesterday. They were also told to be ready to leave here on next Tuesday's transport. Mischa wanted to rush straight to the commandant and call him a murderer. We'll have to watch him carefully. Outwardly, Father appears very calm. But he would have gone to pieces in a matter of days in these vast barracks if

I hadn't been able to have him taken to the hospital—which he is gradually coming to find just as intolerable. He is really at his wits' end, though he tries not to show it. My prayers, too, aren't going quite right. I know: you can pray God to give people the strength to bear whatever comes. But I keep repeating the same prayer: "Lord, make it as short as possible." And as a result I am paralyzed. I would like to pack their cases with the best things I can lay my hands on, but I know perfectly well that they will be stripped of everything; about that we have been left in no doubt. So why bother?

I have a good friend here.[53] Last week he was told to keep himself in readiness for transport. When I went to see him, he stood straight as an arrow, face calm, rucksack packed beside his bed. We didn't mention his leaving, but he did read me various things he had written, and we talked a little philosophy. We didn't make things hard for each other with grief about having to say good-bye. We laughed and said we would see each other soon. We were both able to bear our lot. And that's what is so desperate about this place: most people are not able to bear their lot, and they load it onto the shoulders of others. And that burden is more likely to break one than one's own.

Yes, I feel perfectly able to bear my lot, but not that of my parents. This is the last letter I'll be allowed to write for a while. This afternoon our identity cards were taken away and we became official camp inmates. So you'll have to have a little patience waiting for news of me.

Perhaps I will be able to smuggle a letter out now and then.

Have received your two letters.

'Bye, Maria—dear friend,
Etty

First thing in the morning, before six o'clock, I walk across to Father's barracks, fetch his thermos bottle, then take it to the boiler house: four hot-water taps along the outside wall; a long row of people with bowls, buckets, and coffee-pots; a gentleman with a professorial appearance who controls the traffic. I wait my turn—that little packet of tea from Swiep always in my left-hand coat pocket—burn my fingers at the tap, and the tea has drawn by the time I've walked back. Then to Mother in the hospital (with bronchitis and some exhaustion), fetch her thermos flask, and begin the same pilgrimage. Then to Mischa (who lies three bunks up under a sloping beam in the big barracks, like a prince in disguise) to see if he needs anything.

All the parcels come to me. I try to act fairly as the family rations-distribution center. I walk about with little tin boxes from one person to the other and get real pleasure out of doing it. I simply have no words for the way our friends, including Father's colleagues, are caring for us; sometimes it weighs almost too heavily on my mind. Father is an imperturbable gypsy—just occasionally a decline, during which he would like to step into the freight train and be rid of the whole mess—but he always pulls himself out of it again. He passes his days here with half a dozen little Bibles—Greek, French, Russian, etc.—and keeps surprising me with particularly apposite texts. He is modest in his demands, and lives mainly on bread. On the day before the transport that he was firmly convinced he would be joining, he was as cool as a cucumber, read Homer with his sick boys, and gossiped with former student friends who have turned into gray-haired rabbis.

I learned in good time from an unforgettable friend[54]—

for whose death I still give thanks every day—the great lesson from Matthew 24: "Take therefore no thought for the morrow: for the morrow shall take thought for the things of itself. Sufficient unto the day is the evil thereof." This is the only attitude that allows you to carry on at Westerbork.

And so every night, with sure peace of mind, I lay down my many earthly cares at the feet of God Himself. They are often trivial cares—for instance, how I am going to finish the family wash. The big worries are worries no longer; they have all merged into a fate to which one has been joined. The Puttkammer story has filled me with shame.[55] It shows you just what mad antics people in need will get up to.

But I'm sure there are limits. And a money business like that is certainly not for us. Don't in heaven's name worry your head about it any longer. What tens and tens of thousands before us have borne, we can also bear. For us, I think, it is no longer a question of living, but of how one is equipped for one's extinction.

Dearest Christine,

Your choice collection of goggles is already in place protecting our eyes from the dust, and the other good things
of life have also arrived safely. The little sponge cakes were
unsurpassed. I am putting some of them by in a tin so I
can gladden my father's heart with a couple each day. It's
wonderful to be able to bring him something really delicious from time to time. Please tell Hansje Lansen when
you have a chance that Father isn't able to write back to
her. She sent a moving letter which was very much appre-
ciated; do please tell her. Have a good time in Groningen.
   More later.

'Bye,
Etty

Maria, dear friend,

This morning there was a rainbow over the camp and the sun shone in the mud puddles. When I went into the hospital barracks, some of the women called out, "Have you got good news? You look so cheerful." I considered saying something about Victor Emmanuel, about a popular government, and about peace being on the way.[56] I couldn't fob them off with the rainbow, could I?—even though that was the only reason for my cheerfulness.

"It's going to come to an end soon, it's all going to come tumbling down," chanted a little old wrinkled professor opposite me at the wooden table. People's spirits are high. Italian sounds blossom between the iron bunks and the rags. There must be a modicum of truth in the reports repeated in conversations here as if through distorting mirrors. An "Aryan" with bullet wounds was brought into the camp and put in a separate corner of one of the hospital barracks. Not long after, a police car with detectives came driving down our muddy little paths, the polo-shirted commandant bicycling in front to show the way. They say that the man with the bullet wounds was interrogated non-stop for hours. But otherwise he was treated with great respect, they say. The commandant fetched from his own house a little cushion for the man. They say that he is a Dutch resistance fighter. They also say that he is the mayor of Beilen. They say that several more Aryans have been brought into the camp, all with bullet wounds. They say that there is great unrest in Drenthe. A few evenings ago a fire blazed against the gray sky over our steppe; I stood watching it for a long time in the rain. The next morning a Jew in green overalls mounted guard in front of the barracks opposite the orphanage, where the children play on a small piece of sandy ground surrounded by barbed wire. Green Overalls was guarding twenty non-Jews: men, women, children, picked up in the middle of the night from their beds in Drenthe as hostages because of the fire. (Privately, resentment was expressed by some inmates that we should have to keep watch over non-Jews in a Jewish camp.) But that very same day, the twenty all vanished again.

Yesterday we had a general come to visit us. We were driven from our beds at the crack of dawn. A fever of spring-cleaning burst out in the camp; for a few hours I wandered homeless through the mud. The patients in the hospital had to keep to their beds, the food appeared to be somewhat better than usual, the patients in the large barracks had to have stars sewn on their pajamas, and no one was allowed to wear a loose star. A fat toad in a green uniform—surely the general—shuffled about between the barracks. They say that he came because there is so much unrest in Drenthe. Spirits here are very high. For a few weeks now no transports have left, and it looks as if no more will be leaving. So they say. This place will be turned into a labor camp with a concentration camp as an annex. The people in the punishment barracks, whose number is growing every day, will have to have their heads shaved and wear prison uniform. They don't know what to do with the old people and the children; no ruling has been made about them yet. The commandant has decided that they will be allowed to stay on. So they say. My father is lying sick in a shed with 130 people. "The Lower Depths," [57] he chuckles. He chuckles a great deal. Little Bibles in various languages and French novels are strewn all over his untidy blankets. His suit, his winter coat, all his wordly goods are lying crumpled in a heap behind his pillow. The men's beds

have been put right next to each other. The "brothers"—
the male nurses—walk quickly past; God forbid you
should ask them anything. "You have to be as fit as a fiddle
to survive in this hospital," says Father, "if you're sick you
haven't a hope." For a few days he was really ill, with a
temperature of about 104°F and diarrhea. I toast bread for
him at Anne-Marie's and keep running to the boilerhouse
to fetch hot water for tea. I barter rye bread for rusks and
other easily digestible things; I'm doing a roaring trade in
rye bread. Yesterday a kind lady brought him a royal gift:
a roll of toilet paper. She is the wife of a leading rabbi who
works here in the charity department. Father thanked her
with extreme courtesy. I often slip in to see him; it always
means a minor battle with the doorkeeper, who is a stickler
for the rules. Father once forgot himself to the point of
calling him a *Feldwebel*.[58] Almost bursting into tears, the
man said in a strong German accent, "But look, mister,
I've been living in Holland for the past ten years." "And I
for three hundred," Father answered tersely. But next day
he wanted to make it up: he said, "I didn't mean to insult
you or any *Feldwebel*." Anyway, that doorkeeper takes up
too much of my cunning and energy. We chuckle together
a lot, Father and I; you can't really call it laughing. He has
a primitive sense of humor, which becomes more profound
and sparkling as the grotesque process of his reduction to
poverty assumes ever more wretched dimensions.

They still do not realize, my God, that apart from You,
everything here is quicksand. That just slipped out.

I'm sitting in one of the big barracks at a wooden table,
three bunks behind my back, three bunks in front of me.
The barracks is like some colorful, sultry back street in the

Orient. People shuffle along the narrow pathways between bunks. A little old woman asks, "Can you tell me where So-and-So lives?" "At number so-and-so," says Mechanicus, who is sitting next to me and writing, a sort of tramp's trilby hat on his head against the flies. Every bunk here has a number, and someone lives at every number. Though it resembles an Eastern bazaar, when I walk between the beds and look out of the open window I see gray Dutch rain clouds, potato fields, and far in the distance, two Dutch trees. Opposite me sits Jo Spier's seventy-year-old father, eternally youthful; he draws rust-brown barracks in a sketchbook. Beside him somebody mutters prayers over a book with Hebrew letters. A raw wind blows through the barracks, several windowpanes are broken, yet the air is stale and foul-smelling. Like an agile monkey, Mechanicus has just clambered up onto his third-tier bunk and triumphantly reappears with a tin of pea soup. A small space has become free on the stove in the washhouse. It is half-past twelve; I am invited to stay on in this Eastern back street on the Drenthe heath to eat pea soup. I have a good life, indeed!

Sunday morning, 8:00 o'clock, 8 August

I've had a wash at the tap in our tiny kitchen and crept back into bed. A huge pan of endives is bubbling away on the little hotplate; the ten of us in our small barracks have a few hours of cooking time first thing this morning. My roommates are domestic women whose lives revolve around that one small hotplate. With comical results, sometimes; mostly enough to make you weep. I am hardly ever at home. We have three books in our little house: *Quicksilver* by Cissy van Marxveldt, *The Divorce* by Henri van Booven, and *Conversations with Sri Krishna*. People almost come to blows for browsing rights to Cissy van

Marxveldt. When I last took out the Bible, one of my roommates said smugly, "I've hidden my own Bible away somewhere safe!" The rain beats against our small windows, it is cold, it looks as if summer is definitely over. From my bunk I can see gulls in the distance moving across the flat gray sky. They are like free thoughts in an open mind.

Last night I went with Mechanicus to see Paul's mother. She found a louse, so for the past few days she has been in the quarantine barracks. Not only did she have the louse; at the same time she had an inoculation and a back tooth pulled. And now she must sit on a narrow little bench and peel potatoes every day for hours. "Slave labor," she says. She is in a bad way. The quarantine barracks looks like a house of correction, without a single object that provides home comfort. The three of us talked about the many parentless children, some of them already like little old men and women, who are herded together outside in the rain every morning, while the barracks are cleaned. We talked about the soul-destroying work of picking peas and beans, about the danger of letting go and becoming demoralized, about all the dreary and grotesque details of camp life. "You can never describe things like that, you can only suffer them," said Mechanicus grimly. He is leaning with his elbows on the wooden table; he has fleas, holey socks, and cold shivers. He remarks with good-natured self-mockery, "This evening I feel just like a very small boy afraid of the wolf." Later I saw him back to his own barracks and took his holey socks home with me. Paul's mother went with us part of the way through the night, a large woollen shawl around her shoulders, her gray hair loose in the wind. Do you still remember that musical afternoon when Paul played the flute in the bay window and his mother sat with such stately dignity in the middle of the room?

. . .

Many feel that their love of mankind languishes at Westerbork because it receives no nourishment—meaning that people here don't give you much occasion to love them. "The mass is a hideous monster; individuals are pitiful," someone said. But I keep discovering that there is no causal connection between people's behavior and the love you feel for them. Love for one's fellow man is like an elemental glow that sustains you. The fellow man himself has hardly anything to do with it. Oh Maria, it's a little bit bare of love here, and I myself feel so inexpressibly rich; I cannot explain it.

In your reply, please don't let it slip that you received this letter outside my writing day—there is strict censorship on incoming mail at the moment. Love to you all.

Etty

Dear Christine,

Best, warmest greetings from us all. I thought I would send this letter, meant for a girl friend, to you first. Much that is in it might easily have been written to you, and this way you'll have more news of us. And when you've read the enclosed pages, will you please forward them to Sister Maria Tuinzing, c/o Heer Wegerif, 6 Gabriel Metsustraat? One Sunday morning she brought you a cup of coffee when you were sitting by my bed, and we spoke about the *Stundenbuch*, do you remember?[59] That *Stundenbuch* now lies under my pillow, together with my small Bible. And yes, the words from Isaiah are magnificent and comforting and time and again give one the secret inner peace that passes all understanding. And what was magnificent as well—and now I am taking a huge jump down to earth— was the little tin of crabmeat and the toast and all the other precious things. We suspect that you gave us not only the best but the last things from your own supplies, and the feeling that arouses in us can't be expressed in words. The parcels from your mother were so sweet, too. And the apples were wonderful—I can't mention everything or I shall run out of paper. We got a very nice letter from Kraak with lots of music in it. We hope you've had a good rest and are going back to work refreshed. Father is a little better, though he's still not allowed to eat much. He is patient enough, the good man, and yet you know, I hope for him (and for so many, many others too) that things won't go on for much longer—

I must bother you again with some mundane requests; I feel awful, but there's no help for it. What we need urgently for Father is rusks and things like that. He hasn't eaten for days and must be helped back to his usual form slowly; the camp bread is terrible. And we have no sugar—we finished what we had, and we don't get any sugar at all here. Is it still possible to get hold of some, down a dark alleyway? At the moment we have no butter either, but it's possible that some will arrive any day from Deventer; you can never tell. That half pound of yours from Amsterdam came exactly when it was needed. Well, the truth is out again: long live material things. We shall all of us bear up, on both sides of the barbed wire, won't we? Things are going well, they say. The rest is in the enclosed letter. Thanks for your goodness and love, dear child. Love to Hansje Lansen.

'Bye,
Etty

[Letter to Maria Tuinzing.]

Later on, when I no longer have to sleep on an iron bunk in a camp surrounded by barbed wire, I shall have a little lamp above my bed so that I can have light around me at night whenever I want. When I lie drowsing, thoughts and little stories often whirl through my brain, as random and transparent as soap bubbles, and I would so like to be able to capture them on paper.

In the mornings when I wake up, I lie cocooned in these stories; it is a rich awakening, you know. But then I get twinges of pain; the ideas and images simply demand to be written down, but there is nowhere for me to sit in peace. Sometimes I walk around for hours looking for a quiet little corner. Once a stray cat came in during the night. We put a hatbox for it on the WC, and it had kittens inside. I sometimes feel like a stray cat without a hatbox.

Tonight Jopie's son was born. His name is Benjamin and he sleeps in a drawer. They have now put some sort of madman beside my father.

You know, if you don't have the inner strength while you're here to understand that all outer appearances are a passing show, as nothing beside the great splendor (I can't think of a better word right now) inside us—then things can look very black here indeed. Completely wretched, in fact, as they must look to those pathetic people who have lost their last towel; who struggle with boxes, trays of food, cups, moldy bread, and dirty laundry, on, under, and around their bunks; who are miserable when other people shout at them or are unkind, but who shout at others themselves without a thought. Or to those poor abandoned children whose parents have been sent on transport, and who are ignored by the other mothers—who have worries enough with their own brood, what with the diarrhea and all the other complaints, big and small, when nothing was ever wrong with them in the past. You should see these poor mothers sitting beside the cots of their wailing young in blank and brute despair.

I have visited ten different places in order to fill this one sheet of paper: my makeshift little table in our workshop; a wheelbarrow opposite the laundry where Anne-Marie works (standing for hours in the heat surrounded by children whose thoughtless screaming she finds very difficult to cope with right now; yesterday I dried her tears but didn't tell her that I was writing it all down—these scribblings to you are meant for Swiep as well); a lecture given last night in the orphanage by a long-winded professor of sociology; a windy bit of "dune" under the open sky this morning—each time I add another few words—and now I am sitting in the partitioned-off hospital canteen, which I have only just discovered, a place to which I shall be able to withdraw now and then for a little while.

Tomorrow morning Jopie leaves for Amsterdam. For the first time in the months I have been here, I feel a small stab in my disciplined heart. Why am I being left behind? But still—everyone's time will come. Most people here are much worse off than they need be because they write off their longing for friends and family as so many losses in their lives, when they should count the fact that their heart is able to long so hard and to love so much among their greatest blessings. Well, dear Lord, I thought I had found a quiet little spot, but it is suddenly full of kitchen staff with clattering pans of stew and hospital staff settling down around the trestle tables to eat. It is past noon and I am off to look for somewhere else.

Had a stab at philosophy late at night, with eyes that kept closing with fatigue. People sometimes say, "You must try to make the best of things." I find this such a feeble thing to say. Everywhere things are both very good and very bad at the same time. The two are in balance, everywhere and always. I never have the feeling that I have got to make the best of things; everything *is* fine just as it is. Every situation, however miserable, is complete in itself and contains the good as well as the bad. All I really wanted to say is this: "making the best of things" is a nauseating expression, and so is "seeing the good in everything." I should like to explain why in greater detail, but if you only knew how tired I feel—I could sleep for fourteen days at a stretch. Now I'm going to take this to Jopie. Tomorrow morning I'll go with him to the police station, and then he is off to Amsterdam, and I back to the barracks.

Well, my children, good-bye!
Etty

Christine,

Today you really were a guardian angel, never have I watched so desperately for a parcel as this week. And now one has come at last, and what a parcel! I took the rusks and rolls straight to Father. The poor soul is thin as a rake after all the fasting; he has an abscess on his eye and a bullying doorkeeper. It's rather sad, but one mustn't dwell on it too much. And yet he is considered the miracle of the barracks: the only person there who can read with concentration—Hebrew, French, Dutch, whatever you like, he goes on reading. No one can understand how any man can do it in such surroundings. You won't mind too much, will you, if I mix things up a bit? I am on night duty again—have to attend to people now and then, and I'm giddy with fatigue. I hope you have heard from me twice: a piece from my letter to Amsterdam and a note enclosing a letter to Sister Tuinzing. I think you must have got the last one, because I'm almost sure that your lavish parcel was a direct response. I am so glad that I can get a short message through, thanks to some brave people. It looks as if our official letters are being held back for the time being. We aren't receiving incoming mail anymore either, it would seem. But keep on writing, please; sooner or later it will get through to us again.

I'm curious to know whether the Jewish Council in Deventer is still functioning. I have heard nothing from them recently. The Gelder family is here. You know that packets can be sent by letter post from the provinces up to a maximum weight of two kilos—best not registered, since the registered parcels are waylaid. There's always a new rule here. Should they forbid all contact with the provinces, then it would probably be best for you to get in touch with

Mevrouw M. Kuiper, 61 Reynier Vinkeleskade, Amsterdam, who looks after all sorts of luggage for us via the Amsterdam Jewish Council. We are causing you a lot of trouble, aren't we? Oh Christine, I mustn't even think about it, this week I really saw what a misery it all is. I was so touched to get the tea, and the butter was a gift straight from heaven. We had run out of it for a few days; that's not such a dramatic event in itself—after the war began, I often ran out of butter for a few days in Amsterdam—but everything is so much worse here, particularly since people are so debilitated by illnesses and minor complaints and the bad climate. Physically Father isn't all that well at the moment, and by way of a change, Mother is beginning to suffer with bladder trouble.

Will you think badly of me if I make more requests? Could you get some little Antifones at a chemist's? They're the things you put in your ears to block out noise. In Mother's barracks it is very noisy at night, with a lot of small children who are sick—really there's nowhere here that isn't noisy—and now she wants to try sleeping with earplugs.

And again: do you know a product called Reformite? It's something like Marmite, and you spread it on bread. It has helped to keep Mother's appetite up. There is a peculiar kind of disease here: for days on end a person feels not the slightest need for food. It's a mad place, this. And now one more thing: it appears that there may still be some of our lard left at Brian's. If you could send us a small chunk now and then, I could probably fry some potatoes on a hotplate belonging to some friends. And that's enough requests; they're making me feel ill.

Now I'm going to send you something nice too, something I've just read about Paula Modersohn-Becker: "A deeply unexpectant attitude toward life was in her blood, something that was, in fact, a genuine expression of a supreme expectation: disregard of all things external thanks to an instinctive perception of one's own riches, and a secret, not entirely explicable, inner happiness."

Father wants to write to you on his writing day, but it may not be sent through. Oh well, the bonds that exist between people can't be broken by small setbacks. Start your new course in good heart, and think of us now and then.

We send you our love.

Etty

Darling Tide,

I thought at first I would give my writing a miss today, because I'm so terribly tired, and also because I thought I had nothing to say just now. But of course I have a great deal to write about. I shall allow my thoughts free rein; you are bound to pick them up anyway. This afternoon I was resting on my bunk and suddenly I just had to write these few words in my diary, and I now send them to you:

"You have made me so rich, oh God, please let me share out Your beauty with open hands. My life has become an uninterrupted dialogue with You, oh God, one great dialogue. Sometimes when I stand in some corner of the camp, my feet planted on Your earth, my eyes raised toward Your heaven, tears sometimes run down my face, tears of deep emotion and gratitude. At night, too, when I lie in my bed and rest in You, oh God, tears of gratitude run down my face, and that is my prayer. I have been terribly tired for several days, but that too will pass. Things come and go in a deeper rhythm, and people must be taught to listen; it is the most important thing we have to learn in this life. I am not challenging You, oh God, my life is one great dialogue with You. I may never become the great artist I would really like to be, but I am already secure in You, God. Sometimes I try my hand at turning out small profundities and uncertain short stories, but I always end up with just one single word: God. And that says everything and there is no need for anything more. And all my creative powers are translated into inner dialogues with You. The beat of my heart has grown deeper, more active, and yet more peaceful, and it is as if I were all the time storing up inner riches."

Inexplicably, Jul has been floating above this heath of

late.[60] He teaches me something new every day. There are many miracles in a human life. My own is one long sequence of inner miracles, and it's good to be able to say so again to somebody. Your photograph is in Rilke's *Stundenbuch*, next to Jul's photograph. They lie under my pillow together with my small Bible. Your letter with the quotations has also arrived. Keep writing, please, and fare you well, my dear.

Etty

[undated, after 18 August 1943]

Now, that is something I can't say to the young mothers with their babies, women who will probably be riding straight to hell in a bare freight train. They would reply, "It's easy for you to talk, you haven't got any children," but that really has nothing to do with it.

There is a passage in the Bible from which I always draw new strength. I think it goes something like: "He that loveth me, let him forsake his father and mother." Last night I had to struggle again not to be overwhelmed by pity for my parents, since it would paralyze me if I gave in to it. I know that we must not lose ourselves so completely in grief and concern for our families that we have little thought or love left for our neighbors. More and more I tend toward the idea that love for everyone who may cross your path, love for everyone made in God's image, must rise above love for blood relatives. Please don't misunderstand me. It may seem unnatural—And I see that it is still far too difficult for me to write about, though so simple to live—

This evening Mechanicus and I will visit Anne-Marie and her long-standing host, the barracks leader, who has a little room of his own. We shall be sitting in what passes in Westerbork for a large apartment, with a big, low window that stands open; and the heath outside the window is as vast and rolling as the sea. It's where I wrote my letters to you last year. Anne-Marie will no doubt make the coffee, and our host will talk about camp life in the early days (he has already been here five years), and Philip will write short stories about it all. I shall delve into my little tins to see if there is anything good to eat with some coffee; and who knows, little Etty, perhaps Anne-Marie will have made another pudding, like that unforgettable almond pudding she served up last time. It was hot today; it will be a lovely summer evening in front of that open window and the heath. Later on, Philip and I will leave and find Jopie. A peaceful trio, we shall then go for a walk around the great gray Bedouin tent that rises up from a broad stretch of sand. They used to put people with lice in it; now it houses stolen Jewish household goods that will ultimately adorn the commandant's house or go to Germany as "gift parcels." A different sunset is staged every night in the sky behind the tent. There are many landscapes in this camp on the Drenthe heath. I believe the world is beautiful all over, even the places that geography books describe as barren and dull. Most books are no good, really; we shall have to rewrite them all—

I wrote my fortnightly letter to Tide; we are only allowed to write on one side of the page now—

My children, how did you manage to come by something as princely as that half-pound of butter? I got the fright of my life, it was colossal. Please forgive this materialistic ending. It is half-past six. Now I must go and pick up the family's bit of food.

My fondest, fondest love to you all.

Etty

[Postcard to Christine van Nooten, 19 August]

Many thanks for
multifarious parcel!

Etty

Sunday morning, 22 August 1943

A pampered nine-month-old baby, a little girl, lies in the maternity ward here. Something very sweet, blue-eyed, and beautiful. She arrived here a few months ago with a "criminal record," for the police had found her abandoned in a clinic. No one knows who or where her parents are. The baby has been in the maternity ward here for so long that the nurses have become very fond of her, and treat her like a little plaything. But what I wanted to tell you is this: when she first came, the baby was not allowed out. All the others were put out in the fresh air in prams, but this one had to stay inside, for after all, she had a criminal record. I checked this with three different nurses, because I found it so hard to believe, even though the strangest things happen here all the time, and they all confirmed the story.

I met a slightly built, undernourished twelve-year-old girl in the hospital barracks. In the same chatty and confiding manner in which another child might talk about her sums at school, she said to me, "I was sent here from the punishment block; I am a criminal case."

A little boy of three and a half who broke a windowpane with a stick got a hiding from his father and began to howl noisily, crying, "Ooooh, now I'll be sent to 51 (= the prison), and then I'll have to go on the transport all by myself."

What children here say to each other is appalling. I heard one little boy say to another, "You know, the 120,000 stamp isn't really any good; it's much better to be half-Aryan and half-Portuguese."[62] And this is what Anne-Marie heard one mother say to her children on the heath: "If you don't eat your pudding up straightaway, then Mummy won't be with you on the transport!"

This morning the woman who has the bunk above my mother dropped a bottle of water. Most of it landed on Mother's bed. In this place something like that is like a natural disaster of scarcely imaginable proportions. The nearest thing in the outside world would be a flooded house.

I am getting quite fond of this hospital canteen. It is just like a Wild West log cabin. A low, rough-hewn wooden hut, rough-hewn tables and benches, small rattling windows, nothing else. I look out on a barren strip of sand with unkempt grass, bounded by a high bank of sand thrown up from a ditch. A deserted railway track curves along in front. During the week, half-naked sunburned men push trolleys about out there. From here the view of the heath is quite unlike anything you can see from any other spot in this hole of a place. Beyond the barbed wire is an area of billowy, low shrubs: they look like young spruce. This pitilessly barren landscape, the rough cabin, the sand, the small, stinking ditch—it's all reminiscent of a gold-mining camp somewhere in the Klondike. Opposite me across the rough wooden table, Mechanicus is chewing at his fountain pen. We look at each other now and then over our little scraps of scribbled-on paper. He records everything that happens here most faithfully, almost officially. "It's too much," he says suddenly. "I know I can write, but here I am face to face with an abyss—or a mountain. It's too much."

The place is beginning to get crowded again as people with threadbare hand-me-downs and the right stamps sit down to eat turnips out of enamel bowls.

Later

Elly dear, your letter made me very happy and said a great deal to me.

Jopie brought a vivid reminder of you all back with him. It was doubly welcome because hardly any mail has been allowed through recently. As far as letters are concerned, we are just about cut off—one of the worst vexations of all. But we mustn't let it depress us; we must try to remain inwardly strong.

Anne-Marie was deliriously happy with *Swiep's* scribbles.

To my regret, the rye bread from *Leonie* ended up in the wrong stomachs. Our bread position, so to speak, was favorable when it arrived, so I hastily distributed it among people whose situation was less favorable. The next day I could hardly ask for perishable goods like that back again; but next time, at least, I'll know who it's for.

So touching, the grapes and pears. Parcels always leave me at a loss; I never can say much. I am, as always, overjoyed with the Sanovite. I save it mainly for Father and Mother, to make a change from the camp bread, which quickly goes moldy. Thank you for the loan of your flashlight, *Father Han;* it's extremely useful in the dark, what with all the puddles and barbed wire.

Jopie told me a breathtaking story about Hans. Each one of us still lives under his own star, it appears. Jopie also said that he kept coming across me in all sorts of nooks and crannies in the old house—that I was with you still.

24 August 1943

There was a moment when I felt in all seriousness that after this night, it would be a sin ever to laugh again. But then I reminded myself that some of those who had gone away had been laughing, even if only a handful of them this time . . . There will be some who will laugh now and then in Poland too, though not many from this transport, I think.

When I think of the faces of that squad of armed, green-uniformed guards—my God, those faces! I looked at them, each in turn, from behind the safety of a window, and I have never been so frightened of anything in my life. I sank to my knees with the words that preside over human life: And God made man after His likeness. That passage spent a difficult morning with me.

I have told you often enough that no words and images are adequate to describe nights like these. But still I must try to convey something of it to you. One always has the feeling here of being the ears and eyes of a piece of Jewish history, but there is also the need sometimes to be a still, small voice. We must keep one another in touch with everything that happens in the various outposts of this world, each one contributing his own little piece of stone to the great mosaic that will take shape once the war is over.

After a night in the hospital barracks, I took an early-morning walk past the punishment barracks. And prisoners were being moved out. The deportees, mainly men, stood with their packs behind the barbed wire. So many of them looked tough and ready for anything. An old acquaintance—I didn't recognize him straightaway; a shaven head often changes people completely—called out to me with a smile, "If they don't manage to do me in, I'll be back."

But the babies, those tiny piercing screams of the babies, dragged from their cots in the middle of the night . . . I have to put it all down quickly, in a muddle, because if I leave it until later I probably won't be able to go on believing that it really happened. It is like a vision, and drifts further and further away. The babies were easily the worst.

And then there was that paralyzed young girl, who didn't want to take her dinner plate along and found it so hard to die. Or the terrified young boy: he had thought he was safe, that was his mistake, and when he realized he was going to have to go anyway, he panicked and ran off. His fellow Jews had to hunt him down. If they didn't find him, scores of others would be put on the transport in his place. He was caught soon enough, hiding in a tent, but "notwithstanding" . . . "notwithstanding," all those others had to go on transport anyway, as a deterrent, they said. And so, many good friends were dragged away by that boy. Fifty victims for one moment of insanity. Or rather: he didn't drag them away—our commandant did, someone of whom it is sometimes said that he is a gentleman. Even so, will the boy be able to live with himself, once it dawns on him exactly what he's been the cause of? And how will all the other Jews on board the train react to him? That boy is going to have a very hard time. The episode might have been overlooked, perhaps, if there hadn't been so much unnerving activity over our heads that night. The commandant must have been affected by that too. "*Donnerwetter*, some flying tonight!" I heard a guard say as he looked up at the stars.

People still harbor such childish hopes that the transport won't get through. Many of us were able from here to watch the bombardment of a nearby town, probably Em-

125

den. So why shouldn't it be possible for the railway line to be hit too, and for the train to be stopped from leaving? It's never been known to happen yet. But people keep hoping it will, with each new transport and with never-flagging hope . . .

The evening before, I had walked through the camp. People were grouped together between the barracks under a gray, cloudy sky. "Look, that's just how people behave after a disaster, standing about on street corners discussing what's happened," my companion said to me. "But that's what makes it so impossible to understand," I burst out. "This time, it's *before* the disaster!"

Whenever misfortune strikes, people have a natural instinct to lend a helping hand and to save what can be saved. Tonight I shall be helping to dress babies and to calm mothers—and that is all I can hope to do. I could almost curse myself for that. For we all know that we are yielding up our sick and defenseless brothers and sisters to hunger, heat, cold, exposure, and destruction, and yet we dress them and escort them to the bare cattle cars—and if they can't walk, we carry them on stretchers. What is going on, what mysteries are these, in what sort of fatal mechanism have we become enmeshed? The answer cannot simply be that we are all cowards. We're not that bad. We stand before a much deeper question . . .

In the afternoon I did a round of the hospital barracks one more time, going from bed to bed. Which beds would be empty the next day? The transport lists are never published until the very last moment, but some of us know well in advance that our names will be down. A young girl called me. She was sitting bolt upright in her bed, eyes wide open. This girl has thin wrists and a peaky little face. She is partly paralyzed, and has just been learning to walk again, between two nurses, one step at a time. "Have you heard? I have to go." We look at each other for a long moment. It is as if her face has disappeared; she is all eyes. Then she says in a level, gray little voice, "Such a pity, isn't it? That everything you have learned in life goes for nothing." And, "How hard it is to die." Suddenly the unnatural rigidity of her expression gives way and she sobs, "Oh, and the worst of it all is having to leave Holland!" And, "Oh, why wasn't I allowed to die before . . ." Later, during the night, I saw her again, for the last time.

There was a little woman in the washhouse, a basket of dripping clothes on her arm. She grabbed hold of me; she looked deranged. A flood of words poured over me: "That isn't right, how can that be right? I've got to go and I won't even be able to get my washing dry by tomorrow. And my child is sick, he's feverish, can't you fix things so that I don't have to go? And I don't have enough things for the child, the rompers they sent me are too small, I need the bigger size, oh, it's enough to drive you mad. And you're not even allowed to take a blanket along, we're going to freeze to death, you didn't think of that, did you? There's a cousin of mine here, he came here the same time I did, but he doesn't have to go, he's got the right papers. Couldn't you help me to get some too? Just say I don't have to go, do you think they'll leave the children with their mothers, that's right, you come back again tonight, you'll help me then, won't you, what do you think, would my cousin's papers . . . ?"

If I were to say that I was in hell that night, what would I really be telling you? I caught myself saying it aloud in the night, aloud to myself and quite soberly, "So that's what hell is like." You really can't tell who is going and who isn't this time. Almost everyone is up, the sick help each other to get dressed. There are some who have no clothes at all, whose luggage has been lost or hasn't arrived yet.

127

Ladies from the "Welfare" walk about doling out clothes, which may fit or not, it doesn't matter so long as you've covered yourself with something. Some old women look a ridiculous sight. Small bottles of milk are being prepared to take along with the babies, whose pitiful screams punctuate all the frantic activity in the barracks. A young mother says to me almost apologetically, "My baby doesn't usually cry; it's almost as if he can tell what's happening." She picks up the child, a lovely baby about eight months old, from a makeshift crib and smiles at it. "If you don't behave yourself, Mummy won't take you along with her!" She tells me about some friends. "When those men in green came to fetch them in Amsterdam, their children cried terribly. Then their father said, 'If you don't behave yourselves, you won't be allowed to go in that green car, this green gentleman won't take you.' And that helped—the children calmed down." She winks at me bravely, a trim, dark little woman with a lively, olive-skinned face. She is dressed in long gray trousers and a green woollen sweater. "I may be smiling," she says, "but I feel pretty awful." The little woman with the wet washing is on the point of hysterics. "Can't you hide my child for me? Go on, please, won't you hide him, he's got a high fever, how can I possibly take him along?" She points to a little bundle of misery with blond curls and a burning, bright-red little face. The child tosses about in his rough wooden cot. The nurse wants the mother to put on an extra woollen sweater, tries to pull it over her dress. She refuses. "I'm not going to take anything along, what use would it be? . . . my child." And she sobs, "They take the sick children away and you never get them back."

Then a woman comes up to her, a stout working-class woman with a kindly snub-nosed face, draws the desperate mother down with her on the edge of one of the iron bunks, and talks to her almost crooningly. "There now,

... Jew, aren't you? So you'll just have

... ng I suddenly catch sight of the
... e of a colleague. She is squatting be-
... dying woman who has swallowed some
... no happens to be her mother . . .

"... lmighty, what are You doing to us?" The words
... escape me. Over there is that affectionate little woman
from Rotterdam. She is in her ninth month. Two nurses
try to get her dressed. She just stands there, her swollen
body leaning against her child's cot. Drops of sweat run
down her face. She stares into the distance, a distance into
which I cannot follow her, and says in a toneless, worn-out
voice, "Two months ago I volunteered to go with my husband to Poland. And then I wasn't allowed to, because I
always have such difficult pregnancies. And now I do have
to go . . . just because someone tried to run away tonight."
The wailing of the babies grows louder still, filling every
nook and cranny of the barracks, now bathed in ghostly
light. It is almost too much to bear. A name occurs to me:
Herod.

On the stretcher on the way to the train, her labor pains
begin, and we are allowed to carry the woman to the hospital instead of to the freight train—which, this night,
seems a rare act of humanity . . .

I pass the bed of the paralyzed girl. The others have
helped to dress her. I never saw such great big eyes in such
a little face. "I can't take it all in," she whispers to me. A
few steps away stands my little hunchbacked Russian
woman; I told you about her before. She stands there as if
spun in a web of sorrow. The paralyzed girl is a friend of
hers. Later she said sadly to me, "She doesn't even have a
plate, I wanted to give her mine, but she wouldn't take it.
She said, 'I'll be dead in ten days anyway, and then those
horrible Germans will get it.'"

She stands there in front of me, a green silk
wrapped around her small, misshapen figure. She
very wise, bright eyes of a child. She looks at me for
time in silence, searchingly, and then says, "I would
oh, I really would like, to be able to swim away in
tears." And "I long so desperately for my dear mother
(Her mother died a few months ago from cancer, in the
washroom near the WC. At least she was left alone there
for a moment, left to die in peace.) She asks me with her
strange accent in the voice of a child that begs for forgive-
ness, "Surely God will be able to understand my doubts in
a world like this, won't He?" Then she turns away from
me, in an almost loving gesture of infinite sadness, and
throughout the night I see the misshapen, green, silk-clad
figure moving between the beds, doing small services for
those about to depart. She herself doesn't have to go, not
this time, anyway . . .

I'm sitting here squeezing tomato juice for the babies. A
young woman sits beside me. She appears ready and eager
to leave, and is beautifully turned out. It is something like
a cry of liberation when she exclaims, arms flung wide,
"I'm embarking on a wonderful journey; I might find my
husband." A woman opposite cuts her short bitterly. "I'm
going as well, but I certainly don't think it's wonderful." I
remembered admitting the young woman beside me. She
has been here only a few days and she came from the punishment block. She seems so level-headed and indepen-
dent, with a touch of defiance about her mouth. She has
been ready to leave since the afternoon, dressed in a long
pair of trousers and a woollen sweater and cardigan. Next
to her on the floor stands a heavy rucksack and a blanket
roll. She is trying to force down a few sandwiches. They
are moldy. "I'll probably get quite a lot of moldy bread to
eat," she laughs. "In prison I didn't eat anything at all for
days." A bit of her history in her own words: "My time

wasn't far off when they threw me into prison. And the taunts and the insults! I made the mistake of saying that I couldn't stand, so they made me stand for hours, but I managed it without making a sound." She looks defiant. "My husband was in the prison as well. I won't tell you what they did to him! But my God, he was tough! They sent him through last month. I was in my third day of labor and couldn't go with him. But how brave he was!" She is almost radiant.

"Perhaps I shall find him again." She laughs defiantly. "They may drag us through the dirt, but we'll come through all right in the end!" She looks at the crying babies all around and says, "I'll have good work to do on the train, I still have lots of milk."

"What, you here as well?" I suddenly call out in dismay. A woman turns and comes up between the tumbled beds of the poor wailing babies, her hands groping around her for support. She is dressed in a long, black, old-fashioned dress. She has a noble brow and white, wavy hair piled up high. Her husband died here a few weeks ago. She is well over eighty, but looks less than sixty. I always admired her for the aristocratic way in which she reclined on her shabby bunk. She answers in a hoarse voice, "Yes, I'm here as well. They wouldn't let me share my husband's grave."

"Ah, there she goes again!" It is the tough little ghetto woman, who is racked with hunger the whole time because she never gets any parcels. She has seven children here. She trips pluckily and busily about on her little short legs. "All I know is, I've got seven children and they need a proper mother, you can be sure of that!"

With nimble gestures she is busy stuffing a jute bag full of her belongings.

"I'm not leaving anything behind; my husband was sent through here a year ago, and my two oldest boys have been through as well." She beams. "My children are real trea-

131

sures!" She bustles about, she packs, she's busy, she has a kind word for everyone who goes by. A plain, dumpy ghetto woman with greasy black hair and little short legs. She has a shabby, short-sleeved dress on, which I can imagine her wearing when she used to stand behind the washtub, back in Jodenbreestraat. And now she is off to Poland in the same old dress, a three days' journey with seven children. "That's right, seven children, and they need a proper mother, believe me!"

You can tell that the young woman over there is used to luxury and that she must have been very beautiful. She is a recent arrival. She had gone into hiding to save her baby. Now she is here, through treachery, like so many others. Her husband is in the punishment barracks. She looks quite pitiful now. Her bleached hair has black roots with a greenish tinge. She has put on many different sets of underwear and other clothing all on top of one another—you can't carry everything by hand, after all, particularly if you have a little child to carry as well. Now she looks lumpy and ridiculous. Her face is blotchy. She stares at everyone with a veiled, tentative gaze, like some defenseless and abandoned young animal.

What will this young woman, already in a state of collapse, look like after three days in an overcrowded freight car with men, women, children, and babies all thrown together, bags and baggage, a bucket in the middle their only convenience?

Presumably they will be sent on to another transit camp, and then on again from there.

We are being hunted to death all through Europe . . .

I wander in a daze through other barracks. I walk past scenes that loom up before my eyes in crystal-clear detail, and at the same time seem like blurred age-old visions. I see a dying old man being carried away, reciting the Sh'ma to himself[64] . . .

Slowly but surely six o'clock in the morning has arrived. The train is due to depart at eleven, and they are starting to load it with people and luggage. Paths to the train have been staked out by men of the *Ordedienst*, the Camp Service Corps. Anyone not involved with the transport has to keep to barracks. I slip into one just across from the siding. "There's always been a splendid view from here," I hear a cynical voice say. The camp has been cut in two halves since yesterday by the train: a depressing series of bare, unpainted freight cars in the front, and a proper coach for the guards at the back. Some of the cars have paper mattresses on the floor. These are for the sick. There is more and more movement now along the asphalt path beside the train.

Men from the "Flying Column" in brown overalls are bringing the luggage up on wheelbarrows. Among them I spot two of the commandant's court jesters: the first is a comedian and a songwriter. Some time ago his name was down, irrevocably, for transport, but for several nights in a row he sang his lungs out for a delighted audience, including the commandant and his retinue. He sang *"Ich kann es nicht verstehen, dass die Rosen blühen"* ("I know not why the roses bloom") and other topical songs. The commandant, a great lover of art, thought it all quite splendid. The singer got his exemption. He was even allocated a house, where he now lives behind red-checked curtains with his peroxide-blonde wife, who spends all her days at a mangle in the boiling-hot laundry. Now here he is, dressed in khaki overalls, pushing a wheelbarrow piled high with the luggage of his fellow Jews. He looks like death warmed over. And over there is another court jester: the commandant's favorite pianist. Legend has it that he is so accomplished that he can play Beethoven's Ninth as a jazz number, which is certainly saying something . . .

Suddenly there are a lot of green-uniformed men

133

swarming over the asphalt. I can't imagine where they have sprung from. Knapsacks and guns over their shoulders. I study their faces. I try to look at them without prejudice.

I can see a father, ready to depart, blessing his wife and child and being himself blessed in turn by an old rabbi with a snow-white beard and the profile of a fiery prophet. I can see . . . ah, I can't begin to describe it all . . .

On earlier transports, some of the guards were simple, kindly types with puzzled expressions, who walked about the camp smoking their pipes and speaking in some incomprehensible dialect. One would have found their company not too objectionable on the journey. Now I am transfixed with terror. Oafish, jeering faces, in which one seeks in vain for even the slightest trace of human warmth. At what fronts did they learn their business? In what punishment camps were they trained? For after all, this is a punishment, isn't it? A few young women are already sitting in a freight car. They hold their babies on their laps, their legs dangling outside—they are determined to enjoy the fresh air as long as possible. Sick people are carried past on stretchers. I almost find myself laughing; the disparity between the guards and the guarded is too absurd. My companion at the window shudders. Months ago he was brought here from Amersfoort, in bits and pieces. "Oh, yes, that's what those fellows were like," he says. "That's what they looked like."

A couple of young children stand with their noses pressed to the windowpane. I listen in to their earnest conversation. "Why do those nasty, horrid men wear green; why don't they wear black? Bad people wear black, don't they?" "Look over there, that man is really sick!" A shock of gray hair above a rumpled blanket on a stretcher. "Look, there's another sick one . . ."

And, pointing at the green uniforms, "Look at them,

now they're laughing!" "Look, look, one of them's already drunk!"

More and more people are filling up the spaces in the freight cars. A tall, lonely figure paces the asphalt, a briefcase under his arm. He is the head of the so-called *Antragstelle*, the camp Appeals Department. He strives right up to the last moment to get people out of the commandant's clutches. Horse trading here always continues until the train has actually pulled out. It's even been known for him to manage to free people from the moving train. The man with the briefcase has the brow of a scholar, and tired, very tired shoulders. A bent little old woman, with a black, old-fashioned hat on her gray, wispy hair, bars his way, gesticulating and brandishing a bundle of papers under his nose. He listens to her for a while, then shakes his head and turns away, his shoulders sagging just a little bit more. This time it won't be possible to get many people off the train in the nick of time. The commandant is annoyed. A young Jew has had the effrontery to run away. One can't really call it a serious attempt to escape—he absconded from the hospital in a moment of panic, a thin jacket over his blue pyjamas, and in a clumsy, childish way took refuge in a tent, where he was picked up quickly enough after a search of the camp. But if you are a Jew you may not run away, may not allow yourself to be stricken with panic. The commandant is remorseless. As a reprisal, and without warning, scores of others are being sent on the transport with the boy, including quite a few who had thought they were firmly at anchor here. This system happens to believe in collective punishment. And all those planes overhead couldn't have helped to improve the commandant's mood, though that is a subject on which he prefers to keep his own counsel.

The cars are now what you might call full. But that's

135

what you think. God Almighty, does all this lot have to get in as well? A large new group has turned up. The children are still standing with their noses glued to the window-pane; they don't miss a thing. "Look over there, a lot of people are getting off, it must be too hot in the train." Suddenly one of them calls out, "Look, the commandant!"

He appears at the end of the asphalt path, like a famous star making his entrance during a grand finale. This near-legendary figure is said to be quite charming and so well disposed toward the Jews. For the commandant of a camp for Jews, he has some strange ideas. Recently he decided that we needed more variety in our diet, and we were promptly served marrowfat peas—just once—instead of cabbage. He could also be said to be our artistic patron here, and is a regular at all our cabaret nights. On one occasion he came three times in succession to see the same performance and roared with laughter at the same old jokes each time. Under his auspices a male choir has been formed that sang "*Bei mir bist du schön*" on his personal orders. It sounded very moving here on the heath, it must be said. Now and then he even invites some of the artistes to his house and talks and drinks with them into the early hours. One night not so long ago he escorted an actress back home, and when he took his leave of her he offered her his hand; just imagine, his hand! They also say that he specially loves children. Children must be looked after. In the hospital they even get a tomato each day. And yet many of them seem to die all the same . . . I could go on quite a bit longer about "our" commandant. Perhaps he sees himself as a prince dispensing largesse to his many humble subjects. God knows how he sees himself. A voice behind me says, "Once upon a time we had a commandant who used to kick people off to Poland. This one sees them off with a smile."

He now walks along the train with military precision, a

relatively young man who has "arrived" early in his career, if one may call it that. He is absolute master over the life and death of Dutch and German Jews here on this remote heath in Drenthe Province. A year ago he probably had not the slightest idea that it so much as existed. I didn't know about it myself, to tell the truth. He walks along the train, his gray, immaculately brushed hair just showing beneath his flat, light-green cap. That gray hair, which makes such a romantic contrast with his fairly young face, sends many of the silly young girls here into raptures—although they dare not, of course, express their feelings openly. On this cruel morning his face is almost iron-gray. It is a face that I am quite unable to read. Sometimes it seems to me to be like a long thin scar in which grimness mingles with joylessness and hypocrisy. And there is something else about him, halfway between a dapper hairdresser's assistant and a stage-door Johnny. But the grimness and the rigidly forced bearing predominate. With military step he walks along the line of freight cars, bulging now with people. He is inspecting his troops: the sick, infants in arms, young mothers, and shaven-headed men. A few more ailing people are being brought up on stretchers. He makes an impatient gesture; they're taking too long about it. Behind him walks his Jewish secretary, smartly dressed in fawn riding breeches and brown sports jacket. He has the sporty demeanor yet vacuous expression of the English whisky drinker. Suddenly they are joined by a handsome brown gundog, where from, heaven knows. With studied gestures the fawn secretary plays with it, like something from a picture in an English society paper. The green squad stare at him goggle-eyed. They probably think—though *think* is a big word—that some of the Jews here look quite different from what their propaganda sheets have led them to believe. A few Jewish big shots from the camp now also walk along the train. "Trying to air their importance," mutters someone behind me. "Transport Boulevard," I say. "Could one ever hope to convey to the outside world what has happened here today?" I ask my companion. The outside world probably thinks of us as a gray, uniform, suffering mass of Jews, and knows nothing of the gulfs and abysses and subtle differences that exist between us. They could never hope to understand.

The commandant has now been joined by the *Oberdienstleiter*, the head of the Camp Service Corps. The *Oberdienstleiter* is a German Jew of massive build, and the commandant looks slight and insignificant by his side. Black top boots, black cap, black army coat with yellow star. He has a cruel mouth and a powerful neck. A few years ago he was still a digger in the outworkers' corps. When the story of his meteoric rise is written up later, it will be an important historical account of the mentality of our age. The light-green commandant with his military bearing, the fawn, impassive secretary, the black bully-boy figure of the *Oberdienstleiter* parade past the train. People fall back around them, but all eyes are on them.

My God, are the doors really being shut now? Yes, they are. Shut on the herded, densely packed mass of people inside. Through small openings at the top we can see heads and hands, hands that will wave to us later when the train leaves. The commandant takes a bicycle and rides once again along the entire length of the train. Then he makes a brief gesture, like royalty in an operetta. A little orderly comes flying up and deferentially relieves him of the bicycle. The train gives a piercing whistle. And 1,020 Jews leave Holland.

This time the quota was really quite small, all considered: a mere thousand Jews, the extra twenty being reserves. For it is always possible—indeed, quite certain this time—that a few will die or be crushed to death on the way. So many sick people and not a single nurse . . .

The tide of helpers gradually recedes; people go back to their sleeping quarters. So many exhausted, pale, and suffering faces. One more piece of our camp has been amputated. Next week yet another piece will follow. This is what has been happening now for over a year, week in, week out. We are left with just a few thousand. A hundred thousand Dutch members of our race are toiling away under an unknown sky or lie rotting in some unknown soil. We know nothing of their fate. It is only a short while, perhaps, before we find out, each one of us in his own time. For we are all marked down to share that fate, of that I have not a moment's doubt. But I must go now and lie down and sleep for a little while. I am a bit tired and dizzy. Then later I have to go to the laundry to track down the facecloth that got lost. But first I must sleep. As for the future, I am firmly resolved to return to you after my wanderings. In the meantime, my love once again, you dear people.

Christine,

My dear, considerate friend, I am sending you one of the two postcards we are allowed. The family is still together so far. Father and Mother are now housed in a large barracks again, so life has become much more difficult. You cannot imagine what such a barracks is like. Father is childishly happy if he is not actually trampled underfoot. He sits on his wooden bench and, while small children crawl all over his back, reads about King Solomon and about love. Me you know about. Mischa is stamping tickets in the bathhouse, with a musical score lying open under the bath tickets. Mother looks after her awkward menfolk and will thank heaven if they are allowed to remain. If. None of the Adelaars is left here now. Will you tell Simon that he doesn't have to send things to the Frank family anymore? And will you thank him for the careful packing and dispatch of so many good things? We voice our wishes and you fulfill them. Please give our warm regards to kind Hansje Lansen. We only wish we could thank everyone personally for everything; it would be so very nice if we could.

It won't be long, perhaps, before you hear something from Maria Tuinzing again. The griddle cakes were lovely and fresh! And to continue on this theme: it's a very good thing that the bulk of the bread and butter arrives at the end of the week here, or at the very latest on Monday, so that we are prepared for any eventuality each time a transport is assembled. The greatest recent family drama: Father's only pair of shoes were missing (to avoid the word *stolen*) one bad night, and now he walks about in a borrowed pair that's too big. It's really pitiful, but never mind, we'll get over that too. We could get over everything here, actually, if only we were allowed to remain in this small country. Oh well. It's gradually becoming quite empty here. And are you taking classes of eager young students again? Father still reads Sallust and Homer with a bright boy who digs ditches in the daytime. Luckily Father has been exempted from picking beans and similar edifying labor; physically he's in no state for that sort of work. There isn't much to tell you this time, my friend. It's an oppressive, gray day. I am sitting on an upturned bed on a patch of grass behind the hospital barracks. Your sister sent us a dream of a Groningen cake. The response to Father's longing for rusks has been touching. The need is no longer so urgent; rye bread would be as welcome again—and perhaps easier? My God, what a lot of trouble we are. Sometime I will write you nothing but lyrical outpourings with never a word on the subject of food, which in fact I find odious. How glorious the Psalms are. Do you think that there is a spare blanket anywhere in Deventer? At the end of a card full of nonsense I send you my love, dearest friend, until the next time. We all send you our love. And best wishes too, please, to Father's colleagues.

Your Etty

E. Hillesum, Bar. 41, Westerbork

My little Maria,

I sent the first half of this letter to Father Han; I hope they both arrive at the same time. The first part is just some journalism, not for you, really. Hello, dear child, how are things? I am longing for a few words. Letters are beginning to get through again. If they are registered, we get them without fail. Please be sure to tell Swiep: he can pass it on to people who know Anne-Marie, who is under a lot of strain because she hasn't heard from any of her friends for some time. Hans's scribble made me happy. Took the note for Reb straight to his parents, since I am not allowed to visit him myself. At the moment he is in the big barracks with my papa, who is back from the hospital again. Spirits go up and down, but humor keeps breaking through. For the old people here, though, it's a macabre business. We have managed to get through another Tuesday. If there is a transport next Tuesday, the chances of keeping them here will be slight. One is consumed worst of all by this tension—tension for others, of course.

When I went into our little office this morning, it was in a terrible mess; it had been requisitioned as a dressing room for the revue. The revue is taking over the whole camp. There are no overalls for people on outside duty, but the revue has an "overall ballet"—so day and night, people sewed overalls with little puffed sleeves for the dancers. Wood from the synagogue in Assen has been sawed up to make a stage. One of the carpenters exclaimed, "What would God say if He knew what His synagogue was being used for?" Marvelous, isn't it: God's synagogue in Assen. Oh, Maria, Maria—Before the last transport, the people who were due to leave worked all day for the revue. Everything here has an indescribably clownish madness and sadness.

I am fine, doing my Russian again every day for an hour, reading the Psalms, and talking with hundred-year-old women who attach great importance to telling me their entire life stories. Really I live here just as I used to with you in Amsterdam: in a community, but also very much for myself. This is possible even when one lives with other people, on them, under them, over them, in the middle of them.

Do you know what I would still love to have here? The blue woollen dressing gown that I got from Hesje and my blue felt hat, which is the most comfortable thing I have for my head. It might be good if I had my blue knitted dress as well; it's fairly cold here sometimes, and in case I should suddenly be put on transport—you never know what will happen. Please don't think me too much of a nuisance—

I would like to make another arrangement with you: each Tuesday I'll send the Nethes a short telegram, "Food for four persons" (nothing to do with hunger); if Father and Mother have gone, then, "Food for two persons." Many of us here will never get over the fact that we allowed our old and our sick to go first. This is a deliberate policy based on the "self-preservation instinct." Father asked a male nurse from the last transport, "How can people who are near death in the hospital be forced to go? Surely that's against all medical ethics." And the nurse answered solemnly, "The hospital gives up the corpses in order to hang on to the living." He wasn't trying to be facetious, he was perfectly serious.

Do you see Tide to talk to, sometimes? Tell her about the registered letters too. I am writing everything in a jumble again and not making much sense. People here often feel strangely tired, and I happen to be so myself this morning. But the letter has to be sent off in a little while, so I'm scribbling away. Please would you be kind enough to mail on or hand on the enclosed letters from Mechanicus? It's thanks to him that I'm able to get this off. Jopie's whole family is now in the hospital; the littlest boy is being kept alive with great difficulty.

How terribly young we were only a year ago on this heath, Maria! Now we've grown a little older. We hardly realize it ourselves: we have become marked by suffering for a whole lifetime. And yet life in its unfathomable depths is so wonderfully good, Maria—I have to come back to that time and again. And if we just care enough, God is in safe hands with us despite everything, Maria.

I myself fail to measure up in every way, of course. I can't cope with the many people who want to involve me in their affairs; I am often much too tired. Please give Käthe a cheerful look from me—and press your cheek to Father Han's for me, too? And do you still get on well together? And please will you give my love to my dear desk, the best place on earth? And to Swiep and Wiep and Hesje and Frans and the others? I can see you in front of me, my dear, and I don't have to say any more.

Etty

I have just heard from Hilde Cramer that registered letters aren't coming in anymore either, so save yourselves the bother. But now and then a small postcard or something still manages to filter through.

And how is Ernst? This morning one of my colleagues said, referring to all sorts of awful practices here: "Each moment of your life that your courage fails is a lost moment." And now I am going to the hairdresser. And it's possible that next we shall have to move from our little house into one of the big barracks; five minutes is all the warning you get for anything. This morning I spoke to Liesl Levie; she suffers from dizziness all the time, and says, *"Ich schwindle durch."* [65] Werner's mother has been sent through.

'Bye, my dear,
Etty

Christine,

Opening the Bible at random I find this: "The Lord is my high tower." I am sitting on my rucksack in the middle of a full freight car. Father, Mother, and Mischa are a few cars away. In the end, the departure came without warning. On sudden special orders from the Hague. We left the camp singing, Father and Mother firmly and calmly, Mischa too. We shall be traveling for three days. Thank you for all your kindness and care. Friends left behind will still be writing to Amsterdam; perhaps you will hear something from them. Or from my last letter from camp.

> Good-bye for now from the four of us.
> *Etty*

This card, thrown out of the train by Etty on 7 September, was found by farmers outside Westerbork camp and posted by them.

Etty Hillesum died in Auschwitz on 30 November 1943.

NOTES

1. This undated note was apparently written in the summer of 1942, as Etty was preparing to leave Amsterdam.
2. The house on Gabriel Metsustraat belonged to Han Wegerif (whom Etty, his lover, called "Father Han" or "Papa Han"). Etty herself lived there, together with the German cook Käthe, the nurse Maria Tuinzing, the social democrat Bernard, and Han's son Hans Wegerif.
3. Max Kormann survived the war and rejoined his family in America in 1946. He died in 1962. His son, Professor Gerd Kormann, has kindly provided this note:

"During the Weimar Republic, Max O. Kormann, the son of a Hasidic family from Narol in Galicia, became an active Zionist and in 1927 married Rosa Laufer, a German-born daughter of Jews who had migrated from Galicia into the Rhineland at the turn of the century. The couple took their place among Weimar's many westernized Zionist families who still remained still remained loyal to rabbinic Judaism. When they settled in Hamburg, they joined the orthodox congregation of Joseph Carlebach. Here the rebel from Narol, now a traveling shoe salesman, cultivated his interest in Freud and, perhaps influenced by Rabbi Carlebach, became a devotee of Maimonides. Although Max spoke Yiddish and Hebrew, the language of the home was German. By the time Hitler became Chancellor of the Republic, there were two sons, who were being reared as modern religous Zionists.

"The sons called him Pappi. To everyone else he was Max—to everyone, that is, except officials, who insisted on using the name represented by his middle initial. From the moment he illegally crossed the Polish frontier, his papers identified him as Osias Kormann, the name he had taken from an older brother who had fallen during the war. Polish, German, and Dutch authorities insisted on Osias, a name without meaning to those who loved him and among whom he lived and worked. It was the name used by the Hamburg policeman who awoke Max and his family on the morning of 28 October 1938, to inform him that he must leave Germany in twenty-four hours. And by other officials—the German who authorized his deportation to Poland; the clerks who approved his one-month return to Hamburg; the shipping-line employees who, while he was separated from his family, helped him embark on the S.S. St. Louis for its vain journey to Cuba and, when Cuba refused to accept the Jewish passengers, back to Europe; the Dutch officials who accepted the ship's refugees for internment in Holland; the Westerbork authorities who in 1939 turned him into a founding inmate, and then into a minor official of a new kind of prison; and the German occupiers who assumed direct command over Westerbork in 1942, the year Etty Hillesum arrived as a representative of Amsterdam's Jewish Council.

"She dared to call him Osias, and he accepted this use of the name as a term of endearment. Thus they gave new meaning to a name that had been only official. Together they marked a friendship in a Holocaust that had cut him off, apparently forever, from the ties that bound him to a devoted family desperately waiting in America, now also at war. Before she returned to Westerbork for the last time in 1943, Etty could not have seen him often. After her initial stays in Westerbork she returned to Amsterdam for several months. There my father, who could obtain permission to leave the camp, visited her, perhaps only once for a few hours, while she was entertaining some friends. During this winter and spring of 1942–43, most of her letters to him, and some of his to her, were written, sustaining the moment when their souls had suddenly touched between the barracks and the barbed wire."—*Dr. Gerd Korman,* son of Max "Osias" Kormann.

4. "The man who is closest to me" was Julius Spier, founder of psychochirology, the study and classification of palm prints. Born in Frankfurt in 1887, he had been a bank manager, publisher, and singer. Over the years he had discovered a talent for reading hands and palms with remarkable psychological insight; Carl Gustav Jung persuaded him to turn the talent into a full-time profession. Etty consulted him early in 1941 and eventually became his lover. (See *An Interrupted Life: The Diaries of Etty Hillesum, 1941–1943,* Pantheon Books, 1984.) He died in Amsterdam on 15 September 1942, the day the Gestapo came to take him to Westerbork.

5. Rosenberg was Kormann's barracksmate and close friend. Unfortunately nothing more could be found out about him.

6. "Our people" were the Jewish Council, a body formed at the instigation of the Germans in 1941 to represent Dutch Jewry. Etty had a job as an assistant in one of its departments.

7. Joseph Isodoor Vleeschhouwer, known as Jopie, was a close friend of Etty's; his long letter describing the Hillesum family's last day in Westerbork is reprinted in *An Interrupted Life.* He too was transported; he died on 23 April 1945 at Treubitz, after the Germans evacuated Bergen-Belsen. His wife, Cato Cahen, also died at Treubitz.

8. Joseph and Hedwig Mahler, printers, were German Jews who fled from Germany to Holland in 1935. Both were members of a Jewish resistance group in Holland and were killed by the Nazis. I have been unable to identify Eichenwald.

9. "My dear people" were Etty's former housemates at Han Wegerif's house (see note 2).

10. Werner Sterzenbach was the leader of an escape line out of Westerbork camp. Several times he begged Etty Hillesum to escape, but she refused. Sterzenbach and his wife, Alice Sterzenbach-David, survived the war and are living in Germany.

11. Paul Cronheim was a well-known musician and Wagnerian.

12. This is one of the two letters that were illegally published by the Dutch Resistance in 1943. The two women to whom it was sent were the sisters of the Dr. K. mentioned in the first paragraph—probably Dr. Herbert Kruskal, who survived the war and now lives in Israel. Dr. K. asked Etty to write them her impressions of Westerbork; she used his request as an opportunity to detail life in the camp.

13. Westerbork was built in 1939 by the Dutch government's Department of Justice to house the refugees from Germany. Its earliest inmates included Jews who had been incarcerated in Buchenwald and Dachau.

14. The S.S. *St. Louis*, carrying nearly a thousand Jews to Cuba, made its unfortunate voyage in 1939. The ship was finally allowed to dock in Antwerp. Belgium accepted two hundred passengers; the rest were divided among England, France, and the Netherlands.

15. Limburg was a predominantly Roman Catholic province. The reference here is to a public gesture of support for the departing Jews.

16. A group of nuns and priests of Jewish parentage. After a protest against the persecution of the Jews by Archbishop Johannes de Jong on 1 August 1942, the Nazis held a roundup among the cloistered Jewish Catholics. They captured about three hundred nuns and priests. On 2 August, sixty-three Jewish Catholics came to Westerbork; Etty describes them in this letter and in her diary. One of the nuns described is Edith Stein, a well-known mystic writer and philosopher, with whom Etty has often been compared. Stein was killed in Auschwitz on 9 August 1942.

17. The Herengracht is a fashionable street in Amsterdam; its *bocht* (curve) is the most exclusive stretch.

18. Hanukkah: the Jewish festival of lights, commemorating the triumphant resistance of the Maccabees to their Syrian Greek oppressors in the second century B.C.

19. V stands for *Verzorging* ("care"), an organization providing material and food for the camp inhabitants.

20. Osias Kormann gave lessons on Jewish history and festivals at the Westerbork camp school.

21. The *Zentralstelle für jüdische Auswanderung* (Central Office for Jewish Emigration) was set up by the Germans.

22. Het Leven is Amsterdam's red-light district.

23. NIZ: the *Nederlands-Israëlitisch Ziekenhuis*, or Netherlands-Israelite Hospital.

24. Tide: Henny Tideman, a friend in Julius Spier's circle.

25. Etty's father, Dr. Louis Hillesum, a classicist, had been headmaster of Deventer Gymnasium.

26. The man is probably Herman Boasson, one of Etty's friends in the Westerbork hospital, a scholarly man with whom she often had discussions.

27. The green police, or *grüne Polizei*, were the special German police forces, mostly used for round-ups of Jews.

28. Milli Ortmann, friend of Etty, wife of the painter Theo Ortmann, and member of Amsterdam's intellectual and artistic circle. After Theo's death in 1942, she married a non-Jewish man to protect herself from deportation.

29. There was a camp in a castle in Barneveld for a supposed elite of "cultural Jews." Most of those known to have been interned there survived the war. Mischa—the older of Etty's two brothers, who had been a musical prodigy and was one of Holland's best pianists—was an obvious candidate for the "Barneveld option." Milli Ortmann, through the influence of Willem Mengelberg, the Dutch conductor, secured permission for Mischa to go to Barneveld, but he refused unless his parents could go with him. (See also *The Destruction of the Dutch Jews*, by Jacob Presser, published by Dutton in 1969.)

30. Christine van Nooten lived, and still lives, in Deventer, where she taught classic languages at the Stedelijk Gymnasium. She contributed a number of Etty's letters to this volume.

Mrs. van Nooten knew Etty's father in particular, since he remained headmaster of the Deventer Gymnasium until 29 November 1940.

31. Anne-Marie van den Bergh-Riess was born in 1903 in Berlin. Before the war she had married and divorced Herman van den Bergh, a well-known Dutch poet. As a journalist in Paris, she worked with the Russian writer Ilya Ehrenburg, whom Etty admired. Sent to Bergen-Belsen, she was freed by the Russians.

32. Swiep van Wermeskerken, to whom Etty taught Russian, still lives in Amsterdam.

33. Sam de Wolff (1878–1960), economist and politician. A leading socialist, he was able to leave for Palestine in 1944.

34. The Hollandse Schouwburg was the assembly point for the departure of Jews from Amsterdam.

35. Jaap Hillesum, Etty's younger brother, was a doctor working at the Hollandse Schouwburg.

36. Philip Mechanicus, a journalist, kept a diary of the events in Westerbork, published after the war as *In Depôt*. He and Etty were very close.

37. Friedrich Weinreb, an economist and Old Testament scholar, mentions Etty in his memoirs, *Collaboratie en Verzet* (*Collaboration and Resistance*), Amsterdam, 1969.

38. Renate Levie was the daughter of Liesl and Werner Levie, who were friends of Etty's in Amsterdam (see *An Interrupted Life*). Werner, an opera director who had escaped from Germany, died in the last days of the war; Liesl and her children survived.

39. Chirology: see note 4.

40. Mien Kuiper put on concerts and held musical evenings in her house in Amsterdam, at which Mischa Hillesum often played. It was probably at one of these evenings that Etty first met Julius Spier.

41. Julius Simon, born in 1906, was the main contact for the Jews from Deventer who were brought to Westerbork. Simon organized the food parcels, sending two hundred a week for a long time. He escaped to Switzerland in 1943, and now lives in Holland.

42. Klaas Smelik, Sr., a communist and an author, met Etty in Deventer in 1934. He died in Amsterdam in 1985. Jopie is Johanna Smelik, Klaas's daughter, not to be confused with Jopie Vleeschhouwer. (The nickname "Jopie" is given to both sexes.)

43. NSB: the initials of the Dutch Nazi party.

44. Although Mechanicus's departure was delayed, he was eventually sent to his death in Auschwitz.

45. Grete Wendelsgelst was Milli Ortmann's sister.

46. Nathan Söderblom (1866–1931), Swedish theologian, was awarded the Nobel Peace Prize in 1930.

47. *Dienstleiter*s, or section leaders, who were Jewish.

48. Max Ehrlich, Clara (Chaya) Goldstein, and Willy Rosen were famous cabaret entertainers before the war.

49. Professor David Cohen was co-president with Abraham Asscher of the Jewish Council.

50. Gera Bongers, who now lives in Berlin. See also *An Interrupted Life*.

51. Mevrouw Nethe had been Julius Spier's landlady at 27 Courbetstraat in Amsterdam.

52. Dr. Johannes Brouwer was a scholar of Spanish literature and man of letters. He was shot in the war.

53. Philip Mechanicus; see notes 35 and 44 above.

54. The friend was Julius Spier. The lesson Etty learned from him is found not at Matthew 24 but at Matthew 6:34, which Etty quotes from the Dutch Authorized Version.

55. E. A. P. Puttkammer negotiated with the Germans, buying Jewish exemptions with foreign currency. (See *The Destruction of the Dutch Jews*, note 29 above.)

56. On 25 July 1943, King Victor Emmanuel III accepted Mussolini's resignation, bringing Fascism to an end in Italy.

57. Maxim Gorky's play *The Lower Depths* is set in a crowded Moscow flophouse.

58. *Feldwebel* is a German rank equivalent to sergeant.

59. *Stundenbuch: The Book of Hours*, by the German poet Rainer Maria Rilke, Etty's favorite author.

60. Jul is Julius Spier.

61. The first part of this letter is lost, which explains its abrupt

beginning. It probably consisted of four pages (that is, two sheets), since the first page here bears the number 3. But the other side is not numbered, so this page may have been preceded by two sheets, or four pages.

62. Many Sephardic Jews settled in Holland when they were expelled from Spain and Portugal in the fifteenth and sixteenth centuries.

63. This is the second of the two letters (along with the one dated 18 December 1942) published illegally by the Resistance in 1943.

64. *Sh'ma:* "Hear, O Israel: the Lord our God, the Lord is one." This is a line of the prayer said when death is approaching.

65. In German, "*Ich schwindle durch*" is a pun meaning both "I'm dizzy" and "I'll wangle my way through."

True war – now available in paperback from Grafton Books

To order direct from the publisher just tick the titles you want
and fill in the order form.   GF2181

True war – now available in paperback from
Grafton Books

G M Courtney
SBS in World War Two (illustrated) £2.95 ☐
Peter Firkins
From Hell to Eternity (illustrated) £1.95 ☐
Dick Horton
Ring of Fire (illustrated) £1.95 ☐
Dan van der Vat
The Last Corsair (illustrated) £2.50 ☐
The Ship that Changed the World (illustrated) £3.50 ☐
Edwin P Hoyt
The Kamikazes (illustrated) £2.50 ☐
David Irving
The Mare's Nest (illustrated) £2.50 ☐
The Destruction of Convoy PQ17 (illustrated) £2.95 ☐
Laddie Lucas
Wings of War (illustrated) £3.95 ☐
Charles Whiting
Siegfried: The Nazis' Last Stand (illustrated) £2.50 ☐
First Blood: The Battle of the Kasserine Pass 1943
  (illustrated) £2.50 ☐
Gordon Thomas and Max Morgan Witts
Ruin from the Air: The Atomic Mission to Hiroshima
  (illustrated) £2.95 ☐
James Lucas
Kommando £2.95 ☐
William Seymour
British Special Forces £3.50 ☐

To order direct from the publisher just tick the titles you want
and fill in the order form. **GF2381**

All these books are available at your local bookshop or newsagent, or can be ordered direct from the publisher.

To order direct from the publishers just tick the titles you want and fill in the form below.

Name _____

Address _____

_____

Send to:
Grafton Cash Sales
PO Box 11, Falmouth, Cornwall TR10 9EN.

Please enclose remittance to the value of the cover price plus:

UK 60p for the first book, 25p for the second book plus 15p per copy for each additional book ordered to a maximum charge of £1.90.

BFPO 60p for the first book, 25p for the second book plus 15p per copy for the next 7 books, thereafter 9p per book.

Overseas including Eire £1.25 for the first book, 75p for second book and 28p for each additional book.

Grafton Books reserve the right to show new retail prices on covers, which may differ from those previously advertised in the text or elsewhere.